CONTINUITY
& INHERITANCE

A Biblical Perspective

Thabani Nyoni

MAPLE
PUBLISHERS

Continuity, Legacy & Inheritance – A Biblical Perspective

Author: Thabani Nyoni

Copyright © Thabani Nyoni (2023)

The right of Thabani Nyoni to be identified as author of this work has been asserted by the author in accordance with section 77 and 78 of the Copyright, Designs and Patents Act 1988.

First Published in 2023

ISBN 978-1-915996-20-6 (Paperback)
   978-1-915996-21-3 (eBook)

Book cover design and Book layout by:
   Maple Publishers
   www.maplepublishers.com

Published by:
   Maple Publishers
   Fairbourne Drive, Atterbury,
   Milton Keynes,
   MK10 9RG, UK

A CIP catalogue record for this title is available from the British Library.

All rights reserved. No part of this book may be reproduced or translated by any form or by any means, electronic or mechanical, including photocopying, recording or by any information storage and retrieval system without written permission from the author.

The views expressed in this work are solely those of the author and do not necessarily reflect the views of the publisher, and the publisher hereby disclaims any responsibility for them.

We live in unprecedented times of human history, and the days ahead offer no respite. Indeed, these are the Last Days! Total darkness lies ahead [II Timothy 3: 1 -5]. Our three enemies – Satan, the flesh and the world are on a rampage to obliterate but fear not! [II Timothy 1: 7]. Genuine Christians have become moving targets—so you better have counted the cost [Luke 9: 23 & 62]. In fact, look up! celebrate, for your redemption draws nigh [Luke 21: 28]. This generation's decadents flood the earth like open sewers; anything and everything goes, and the world has become doubly desensitised. This era's sin is twice the filth of Noah's days [Genesis 6; Matthew 24: 37 – 39], as well as that of Sodom and Gomorrah [Genesis 19]. Right or wrong no longer exists. Compromise has become the norm, and without care or moral compass, each person can do as they please. Nevertheless, where sin increases, God's grace abounds considerably more. God is challenging you and me to be faithful, faith-filled, Spirit filled, Spirit led, trustworthy, responsible, willing, obedient, and to be radiant.

From the throne of God, I sense a demand and urgency for the Body of Christ to initiate a domino effect in every sphere of life, a cumulative effect of stirring people into discovering their primary purpose—to love, to serve and to please God alone, cultivated on the Lordship of Jesus Christ. We are to set off a chain reaction of disciples who pursue nothing less. My quest is for generations to grow from faith to faith. This book is not a Manual or shortcut to success. It does not contain Five Steps to Victory, nor promises to "activate" a "hundredfold blessing."

This book has no recitals of marching through life, without affliction or adversity. Instead, roll up your sleeves and take up your battle station. Endure hardness like the good soldier of Jesus Christ, grit your teeth, teach your fingers to fight, and fight the good fight of faith [I Timothy 6: 12]. Yes, you will sweat, you will bleed, you will cry, and some will even die, but I am here to remind you that, 'weeping may endure for a night, but joy comes in the morning' [Psalm 30: 5b]. Also remember, 'the darkest night is before the dawn'.' You will love people, you will rescue them, and ultimately, you will please God! This book is my encouragement to you; know God personally. Pursue the PRIMARY purpose, and everything else will follow. Be disciplined, be determined, be consistent daily and watch the Holy Spirit use you to become an agent of positive change.

THABANI NYONI

CONTENTS

DEDICATION

I dedicate this book to the three most important people in my life....

Thandi – my sweetheart, my confidant, my biggest cheerleader, and my best friend. Thank you for choosing me, for loving me and for being willing to walk this journey with me. God knew that I needed you. You are forever the girl of my dreams.

Lindi & Jabu – my quiver! My manner of life, and my writings are your platforms. This is the way, walk in it! Follow me, as I follow Christ. Love God with all your being. Live in your sweet spot. Submit to His call and walk in your destiny. Be obedient to Him. Constantly pursue Him passionately, with conviction, with enthusiasm [enthios], with integrity of heart and with skill. Never let anyone or anything distract, deter, intimidate, or manipulate you. Affect your seed, your seed's seed and influence generations for Jesus Christ. I am increasing my decibels together with the vociferous Grandstand [Hebrews 12: 1 – 2] urging you on and will never stop—so finish well and finish strong!

PREFACE

I wrote this book over 20 years ago but kept it under wraps, because of the fear of Man. In my eyes, I was a nobody, and was more concerned about what people would say. I sought Man's affirmation and approval – and got none. Caught in this web, I even wondered which 'prominent Man of God' could afford me the courtesy of a foreword. I eventually "woke" up from the fear of Man to an overwhelming reverential fear of God. The Bible is full of truths which we are all going to have to embrace and walk in if we are going to live fulfilled lives here on earth.

Proverbs 29: 25 tells us that the fear of Man is a snare—I certainly got trapped and immobilised for years. I was fearful and more concerned about Man's opinion. I certainly was not like Jehosophat in II Chronicles 20 who was initially fearful of Man but immediately turned his heart to God. Thank God for the Holy Spirit who has helped me every step of the way. He reminded me that, if I keep my mouth shut, one day I will have to account for my inactivity. Concerning fear, the Bible also tells us that the fear of the Lord is the beginning of wisdom [Proverbs 9: 10]. Therefore, I fear God and not Man. It is but an itch to scratch when Man judges me! [I Corinthians 4: 3].

Contemporary Church history is plagued with endless lists of ordinary men and women like you and me who came and went. They crept like shadows, vanished faster than a breath, and died without origin or trace. These men and women were self-centred, blinkered, and triggered short-term perpetual vision. Some got consumed by outward appearance, captivated by social class, and some became obsessed with ethnicity. Others grew big egos, became idols, and even developed into superstars. They all got distracted, derailed, were completely detoured from their destiny, purpose, and mandate. Spiritually, they became numb, dumb, and crippled.

It is the overflow of their lives that has been most devastating. Their failure to grasp the responsibility of continuity, legacy, or inheritance has resulted in a perpetual inherent paralysis and generational weakness. They bequeathed an inability to build solid foundations and demonstrated an ineptitude to erect springboards. Furthermore, they birthed a far-reaching barrage of constant failure to stir and regular omission to spur others into more. Each of us now need a paradigm shift and a mindset overhaul to buck this trend.

God is eternal, and likewise, the Church must be established from generation to generation with longevity, permanence, and eternity in mind. People who genuinely know God live lives worthy of imitation. Their foundation is Jesus Christ, where He alone is preeminent [Colossians 1:18]. Like the wind, they follow His direction, they blow gently, and then they disappear, leaving a lasting mark. Their signposts, indelible imprint, and zeal live forever. They love God passionately, are Bible based, faith-filled, and are unequivocally dependent on the Holy Spirit. Their purpose is to love, serve, and please God. In doing so, they affect their sphere permanently.

They live in each moment, ponder, look yonder, invest in multiple generations, and leave a blueprint. They are not afraid or intimidated in handing over or transmitting the baton or mantle. They agitate the waters of life, causing a domino or ripple effect; a state of being continuous, ongoing without interruption, without cessation, without intermission, and without breaking the uniformity. God blesses them, their children, their mentee as well as those who embrace their influence [Psalms 115: 14].

Each generation makes disciples [Mathew 28: 19 - 20], teaches its children of God's mighty acts, and with each successive wave, there is momentum, transfer, and exponential increase [Habakkuk 2: 14]. When they die, their voices live on. Their blood is like that of righteous Abel; though dead, it still speaks [Hebrews 11: 4].

Psalm 25: 12 - 13 says: 'What Man is he that fears the Lord? Him shall He [God] teach in the way that he shall choose. His soul shall dwell at ease; and his seed shall inherit the earth.' I could write a whole book on these two verses. Think carefully: What Man fears God? This is talking about an individual, not a group. The question is what individual fears God? You? Me? Write your name and own this verse, whether you are married or single. God will teach us and walk with us in all our ways, and we will permanently [forever] live with purpose. The precondition or prerequisite is the fear of the Lord. As a result of our willingness and obedience, our seed will inherit or have dominion here on earth [in their sphere of influence] – all the way into eternity. Our seed is not restricted or limited to just our children. This is also about the Seed [Word of God] and how you plant it.

The Word of God is the Seed, and our children and those people in our sphere of influence are also our seed. Both types of "seed" are eternal [forever]. It is said of the Seed [Word of God] that, 'Heaven and earth may pass away, but not the Word of our Lord and Saviour, Jesus Christ' [Matthew 24: 35]. It is then said of the other seed [our children, mentee, and those we get saved], that God has put eternity in each of our hearts [Ecclesiastes 3: 11]. Like the Sower described by Jesus, who went to sow seed, we need to sow the Seed [the Word of God] to our seed [sphere, children]. It takes one individual who fears the Lord to step into the revelation of the two verses in Psalm 25. He or she will trigger an eternal domino-effect. They will combine two eternal "seeds" to the glory of God. Continuity will be triggered, and Biblical eternity birthed.

When you grasp the above, you will understand that God has gone into your future to prepare the way, and in kindness, He follows behind you to spare you from the harm of your past. He has laid his hand over you [Psalm 139: 5]. Furthermore, spiritual, and natural things are created by words. I am challenging each of us to see a brighter, healthier, and stronger Church in the seasons ahead – so confess it! I am urging us to speak in line with the Word. My plea is for each of us to conform to the Word. Proverbs 10: 13 says, "Wisdom is found on the lips of the discerning...." When our words, have aligned to God's, let us position those that follow, so that we allow God to watch over His Word and bring it into manifestation. Proverbs 24: 3 – 4 says, "By wisdom a house is built, and through understanding it is established; through knowledge its rooms are filled with rare and beautiful treasures." Simple; speak life, walk with wisdom, establish with understanding, gain knowledge, and watch God do the rest.

As you read the coming pages and chapters of this book, may the Holy Spirit enlighten and reveal Himself to you. May the below verse of scripture be underpinning everything you read - God be your portion and your inheritance forever, so that those who follow you, will walk in the same rich vein:

Psalm 16: 5-6
Lord, you alone are my inheritance, my cup of blessing. You guard all that is mine. The land you have given me is a pleasant land. What a wonderful inheritance!

This book has been written to ignite and inspire you to think generationally and live with eternity in mind.

WHY CONTINUITY?

John 12: 24 (ESV)
Unless a grain of wheat falls to the earth and dies, it remains alone;
but if it dies, it bears much fruit.

I had the privilege of growing up in the city as well as in the countryside of Zimbabwe. At an early age I quickly learned while in the countryside, that carefully planting into the ground and nurturing tens of kilograms of maize or cotton seed would subsequently yield tonnes of harvest. The first time I read the above verse, it made so much sense. A grain of wheat that falls into the ground has the power to replicate itself many times over! In every generation, God must receive all the glory; Jesus must be enthroned upon every believer's heart. When we think we have arrived, we become that grain of wheat that remains alone. We must die to self and allow Jesus to live big in us. We must remind ourselves, individually and corporately, that it is God who has done great things in us, with us, for us, and through us. When Man applauds us and places us on pedestals, we need to quickly redirect those praises to King Jesus, acknowledge the leading of the Holy Spirit and give thanks to the Father.

Towards the end of 2003, I pondered on some questions that were asked by our Lord Jesus Christ. The questions were: "O faithless generation, how long am I to be with you? How long am I to bear with you? [Mark 9: 19]. Another question is found in Luke 18: 8. Jesus asked, "Nevertheless, when the Son of Man comes, will He find faith on earth?" These questions gnawed and tugged my inner being. I looked at the world around me, I considered the state of the Church and took an honest spiritual audit of myself. Frighteningly, I realised that I could not confidently answer the Lord's questions. Over a long period, I gathered myself, spent time in prayer, wrote numerous thoughts, meditated on the Word of God, and as a result, this book was birthed.

As I pondered on Jesus' questions, I soon realised that when God asks any question, we need to examine ourselves and make sure that we can respond to Him. Can you answer His questions? In his letter addressed to the Colossians [1: 23], Paul encouraged the Church to *continue* in the faith and not shift from the gospel that they had heard. Jude, the brother of James [and a half-brother of Jesus], also appealed to the Church [Jude: 3 - 4] to *contend* for the faith that was once delivered to the Church. Jude further warns how certain people have crept unnoticed into the Church with their own agendas, which ultimately deny the Lord Jesus Christ. Could that be the current state of the modern Church?

Sadly, since I was born again in 1996, I have watched many times over men and women of God come and go. I have witnessed countless people that were called by God. For a season, they walked strong, and then sadly left the Kingdom. One morning during my quiet time in 2003, God told me that if my life impacted people for the next 100 years and then ceased, that would not be a victory in His Kingdom. He told me that I would just be a one era wonder. God challenged me about impacting people for eternity [forever].

When the storm has swept by, the wicked are gone, but the righteous stand firm forever [Proverbs 10: 25]. This verse raises hope, but also challenges us on its application and outworking. Jesus is coming back for a mature, spotless, and beautiful Bride. She must be fully formed in His image. The Church must be ready and expectant of His return, must be radiant, and must have come of age. The Church must no longer be an infant, without an identity crisis, not confused on what She believes, not caught up in division and not fixated with aimless differences. Like five of the ten virgins who were well equipped and waiting expectantly for the Groom [Matthew 25:1 - 13], the Church must be unwavering at His Word, must be full of oil [Holy Spirit], full of faith, and be breathless with anticipation for the King's return. Let us get ourselves, our homes, our community and sphere - the Bride ready, so that She is adorned with beauty and presentable for the return of our Lord and Saviour Jesus Christ. The sad reality is that some of those who have gone before us, missed this. Continuity, legacy, or inheritance did not run at their very core—in their spiritual veins. They did not understand that the righteous are established forever.

Legacy is something transmitted by or received from a predecessor or the past. Similarly, inheritance is the acquisition of possessions, conditions, or traits from past generations. Both legacy and inheritance in our day, have been limited to material possession—buildings, houses, land, cars, and money. The truth is that legacy and inheritance are physical and spiritual. Physical and spiritual realities are both tangible. Note, therefore, you have a spiritual inheritance. I have inherited certain traits or qualities from my spiritual father.

As long as you are alive, you have the potential to pass something on. Legacies and inheritances form foundations and platforms for others to pursue. You are an heir, and in you, are more heirs. Some men and women from yesteryear did not leave platforms or leave enduring impressions for others to sufficiently consume and emulate. Instead, in their era, they became one generation wonders. Others became superstars, idols, and grew big egos. They lived in the exact opposite of Jesus' own words in John 12: 24 [read it!]. They were like that single seed, self-absorbed and self-centered. Perpetuity was not their hallmark and eternity certainly not in their DNA. After their death, their impact gathered dust and was archived. Their vision and foresight were not God aligned, but instead, it was short-term and temporary. Like the grass, they withered and died, and like the flower, their fame and popularity waned and disappeared [I Peter 1:24-25]. Where is their mark today? What is their legacy?

As I wondered and pondered, I realised that a constant start and stop was never part of God's original plan for Man. He did not create us to succeed and then fail, for Him to repeatedly start the cycle. God birthed us for eternity [Ecclesiastes 3: 11a] and incremented us in every aspect. Upon scrutiny of the Word, you will discover that each generation's peak must become the subsequent generation's platform. God expects us to be fruitful; He desires continual harvest. The harvest or fruit must contain seed, resulting in an increase in His anointing. To anoint is to smear or rub with oil. We are to rub against God the Holy Spirit until we look, talk, behave, and smell like Him. The Bible records that although Elisha died, his body still carried the anointing. Let me expand:

In the spring of the year that Elisha died, a man was being buried when a marauding band of Moabites was seen, and in haste, those in the funeral procession dropped the corpse into the grave of Elisha. As soon as the corpse touched Elisha's bones, the man revived and stood on his feet [II Kings 13:20-21]. Dead things [spiritual or physical] must come alive when they encounter us because of the anointing. The anointing was also seen on Paul. When handkerchiefs or aprons that had merely touched his skin were placed on sick people, they were healed of their diseases, and evil spirits were expelled [Acts 19: 12]. The anointing was so strong on Peter, that his mere shadow would heal the sick as he passed by [Acts 5: 15]. The anointing on us must rub-off, onto those around us. It breaks the yoke of those living in bondage [Isaiah 10: 27]. We must begin to think and act generationally. The Church needs a paradigm shift, an authentic counterculture, a change in mindset, and to practically build unshakable foundations. As God is generational, we need to build on Jesus Christ alone - establishing with longevity, permanence, and eternity [forever] in mind.

Now, let us initiate, kick into motion, and set a domino effect that leads to the maturity of the Church. Not for a select few, based on outward appearance, gifts, or talent, but for the Body of Christ coming to full maturity and attainment of all that God has predestined. In our doing, we will affect our sphere permanently [forever]. God desires us to walk faithfully with whole-hearted devotion [II Kings 20: 3b]. Let us walk with integrity of heart, with Godly character, as well as to skill the anointing [Psalm 78: 72].

Let us invest both now and in future generations. Whether the returns on investment are instant or in the future, or whether we see the yields or others reap the benefits, let us invest with forever in mind. We need to be wise foundation builders, bringing our families, communities, and sphere of influence, to a place of maturity in Christ [Colossians 1: 28]. God requires us to lead and disciple. Be an Initiator and Leader. Initiating is embracing the primary purpose of God and then having the ability to lead and influence others. Leaders understand the immensity of their responsibilities. They are passionate, firstly about God, and then people. God always comes first, and people are at the heart of all they do. Like the voice in the wilderness, they are not afraid or ashamed but speak the truth in love. They do not compromise, and they live out their beliefs. They walk with power, clarity, order, and direction, so that fellow disciples walk in the same rich vein. The power to influence is the ability to change or affect disciples or followers. It is to cause changes without forcing [manipulating or intimidating]. A disciple or follower is one who accepts, embraces, adheres, and assists in spreading what they have been taught, thus establishing continuity and longevity.

The Bible is clear that a wise man [an initiator] knows that the Lord is his inheritance, and in God, he places his hope [Lamentations 3: 34]. He knows unequivocally that God is his portion [Psalms 73: 26]. He allows God to build his house [and everything he does], hence his labour is not in vain. The Lord watches over everything he owns and does. A wise man does not waste energy or even dare do things without God. He is not anxious about today or tomorrow, for he knows Whose hand he is in [Psalms 127: 1 - 3]. Because of God, he will leave an inheritance to his children's children [Proverbs 13: 22a]. This is a definitive action with a plan [Habakkuk 2: 2]; he will leave a lasting legacy, transference of something to someone.

Leaving an inheritance is supposed to be something that should occur as naturally as breathing oxygen. It should become involuntary and an obvious occurrence. In Proverbs 13: 22a, it is apparent to me that at least three generations [your generation, your children's generation, and your grandchildren's generation] are supposed to be impacted by you as the absolute minimum.

With the general life expectancy improving, so does our potential for influence. Our rich vein of heritage must be transmitted and flow into eternity. We need a vision, strategy, and plan that is rooted in Christ. A friend from my school days once wrote to me and said, 'A vision with no action or plan is a daydream, and a plan or action with no vision leads to confusion.' The Bible says it this way, 'With no vision, the people run wild' [Proverbs 29: 18]. Our imprint should outlive our physical existence, as we establish with eternity in mind. You and I must be as influential in death as we are when alive. When we have died, and people have read our family history books, they must talk about Christ in us and convey how we emptied ourselves for the benefit of the generations. Each of us must leave a headache for Satan. This is how we will cause the world to be turned upside down [Acts 17: 6] to the glory of God. God will cause our heirs to be like that of the righteous Abel; though dead, his blood still speaks [Hebrews 11].

Everything starts with a foundation. Where no foundation exists, or where foundations are destroyed, what can anyone or even the righteous do [Psalm 11: 3]? Absolutely nothing! Jesus is the everlasting Foundation [Matthew 7: 24 - 27], and if He remains the Foundation of the righteous, they shall live well. So, who are the righteous? The righteous are those who have a right standing with God, those who recognise that they did not earn their position through good works, but those who have died to self, continue to die daily, and are clothed in Jesus Christ, who is our Robe of Righteousness [I Corinthians 1: 30]. They seek first the kingdom of God and His righteousness [Matthew 6: 33], the righteous love God with all their heart, soul, and mind [Matthew 22: 37]. They are acquainted with Him [Job 22: 21] and only do and say what God instructs [John 12: 49]. The righteous are completely sold out to the kingdom's cause and do not have the safety of a backup plan to revert to in case the going gets rough, tough, or topsy-turvy [II Corinthians 4: 8 - 9]. God is preeminent. They are resolute, unflinching, and they know their God [Daniel 11: 32b]. Through Jesus Christ, the righteous are like life-giving trees, they save lives, win souls, and give new life to others [Proverbs 11: 30]. They identify and establish everlasting covenant relationships, so that in their twilight and at their departure from this life, there is continuity.

Continuity is the state of being unrelenting, ongoing without interruption, without cessation, without intermission, and without breaking the uniformity. Like water molecules that are held together by a hydrogen bond forming a definite flow and consistency, continuity is about the right people fitting into their God-given destiny shoes and running with certainty. It is about passing on the mantle or baton. Continuity is not a choice; it is an obligation; it is something we must do - learn from nature! Plants and animals are not taught to reproduce; it is intrinsic. I have also learned just from observing nature that if the saints [the Church] were trees: Some trees can remain evergreen and be without fruit. Remember Jesus and the fig tree [Mark 11: 12 – 25]? Concerning trees that never produce fruit, when the storms of life such as a severe drought come, we can potentially lose those trees forever. The power of continuity is not in the tree, and neither is it necessarily in the fruit. The power of continuity is in the seed [Seed – Word of God]. The tree and fruit carry the potential of continuity. Did you know that in nature not all trees produce fruit and not all fruit contain seed? It therefore means that we can all enjoy fruit, but if that fruit has no seed, we will enjoy just a single harvest - one era!

The power of continuity is in the seed [genes or core]. Seeds will survive the harshest of environments, but when the weather becomes favourable, in their due season, the tree will rise from the Seed. The seed has the power to replicate itself into the tree that carries fruit containing seed, triggering a continual harvest for perpetuity. The seed can also represent people. Did you know that who we are is what we will potentially replicate in the next generation? Think about it, the youth or young people of the 1960s and 1970s, who pursued "free love," and are now largely in positions of authority such as government and political leaders, have in our generation borne an "anything goes generation." This ranges from no longer recognising the two genders of male or female, redefining marriage, promotion of living in debt, to financial chaos… the list is endless. Nature has further reminded us that the seed is like the Word of God, just as in Jesus' parable [Matthew 13 & Luke 8]. The Church cannot function in its fullness without fully embracing the Word of God in its entirety. This Seed [Holy Bible] is uncompromising; it is without error, and it is the complete Manual for Life.

Did you also know that slight internal [genes] alteration or variance, or an external alteration or physical change in habitat, for a plant or animal, can ultimately lead to extinction of the species? For example, if altering genes affects reproduction, invariably, when the last known living type is dead, it ultimately wipes the species. On the other hand, if for example a freshwater fish is thrown into salt water, the reality is that it would probably not live for long and will eventually die. When extinction happens, generations are wiped. You see the word *generation* is made up of two words, *genes* and *generate*.

A *gene* is defined as part of a cell that controls or influences the appearance and growth of a living thing. To *generate* is to produce an effect or to cause something to be produced. You and I will reproduce after our own kind. As followers of Jesus Christ, it means that we must reproduce those whose inner being, hearts, and very core of existence are full of God and power, so that they produce or cause something to be produced that continues to please Him. Similarly, if the Church succumbs to compromise and bows down to worldly or external pressures, we nullify the Word of God and become bearers of an inherent weakness, transmitted into the next generations, ultimately leading to succession of Godless generations.

Continuity needs to be combined with power to become dominant genes in the DNA of the Church. The more we begin to walk in this level of expression, the easier, quicker, better, and more tangible it is for all the saints to know and to walk with God in each generation. We also need to grasp the economics concept of the law of supply and demand. Where there is an abundance of people who are full of faith, full of the Holy Spirit and operate in their sweet spots, there is an aggregation of experiences, which makes it easier for the subsequent generations to catch onto the things of God.

When power is combined with continuity, it will produce an unending, forceful effect. Power is the energy used and the rate at which work is done. The most powerful entity here on Earth is not Satan, it is not a company, and it is not a currency, and neither is it a country. The most powerful entity is the Church because of the Holy Spirit. The Church's power is both *exusia* [Acts 1: 8] and *dunamis* [Mark 16: 17 - 18]— God's vessel. *Exusia* is a Greek word meaning the power of authority; the authority conferred or delegated empowerment that God gives to His saints, authorising them to operate in a designated jurisdiction; to act to the extent they are guided by faith in His revealed word. *Dunamis* is also a Greek word meaning strength and ability, inherent power, power residing in a thing by its nature or which a person or thing exerts and puts forth. It is power for performing miracles. It is also the power and influence that belong to riches and wealth, as well as power consisting or resting upon armies. When the Church begins to walk in this expression, it will gather *momentum* with time, enabling the Body of Christ to come to maturity.

Momentum comprises two words: *moment* is a continuous period. The other word, *quantum*, means the smallest amount of many forms. Therefore, *momentum* is the strength or force that allows something to continue or grow stronger or faster as time passes.

Let me illustrate; when I was 13years old, I loved to run the 400-metre race. This race is not just about speed but also about endurance. It takes skill to compete successfully; gone are the days when all that it took to win the event was speed. Athletes are now taught when to power, when to sprint, when to coast, and when to allow momentum to take them to the finish line. Good trainers teach athletes how to control their breathing. During a race, controlled breathing aids in increasing endurance. Breathing incorrectly can lead to insufficient oxygen supply in the body. A lack of oxygen produces lactic acid, which will affect the muscles and the heart. In this physical race, the difference between winning and losing is marginal.

Spiritually, too, let us also be participants in our race. We must be people who appreciate detail, who are deliberate and completely devoted to God, and also willing to *transfer*. We were not placed on earth to diminish in power over time. The Church must aggregate each passing moment, remember the past, and then be catapulted into the future. We must desire the unseen, the unheard, and the indescribable experiences with God, and ultimately get to the finish line.

To *transfer* means to move out of and into another. It also means to handover or pass from one person to another. The transfer is like the handover of a baton as in a relay in an athletic competition. This book is not just about succession—the coming of one person or thing after another in order, sequence, or in the course of events. It is also about transitioning; the movement or change from one position, state, stage, subject, concept to another. At every transition or change over, improvement must be tangible, faster, better, and superior.

If you know anything about a relay, you will know that the aim is to complete the full distance, with the complement of runners not dropping the baton. If at any exchange the baton is dropped, your team is automatically disqualified from the race. In any relay, the one who has the baton must be willing to hand it over to the next runner. If he is not willing to do it and runs the full distance alone, he not only looks foolish, but the track judges will not only disqualify him but the team. Another obvious characteristic about a relay is that the following runners know at which stage they know they are going to receive the baton. They wait with expectation, and not passively, and each one wants to run his leg and arrive at the point of transition having completely emptied their tank, leaving nothing in reserve.

Each runner runs to his or her strength. For example, in a 4 X 100-meter relay, some runners are excellent bend runners, and others run on the straight. At the end of the race, although only one member of the team crosses the winning line with the baton, it is the team that is celebrated. At the medal ceremony, it is not the last leg runner who stands on the podium; it is the whole team. Each team member receives the winner's medal. At the time of editing this book, the men's world record for the athletic 100 meters race is 9.58 seconds. That time is phenomenal, but I want to show you the impact of what a relay [teamwork] does.

Even though you must transition the baton between individuals with precision and without dropping it, the world record for the men's 4 X 100 meters is 36.84 seconds. This means that each of the four men is running each 100-meter leg at an average speed of 9.21 seconds—that is faster than both, a straightforward individual 100-meter sprint, as well as the 400-meter flat race—the men's record is currently 43.03 seconds. So, either way, lone runners cannot out perform teamwork. As a pupil, I was involved in numerous relays, and one of the first things you are taught is to set a mark a few meters behind you on the track, so that when the preceding runner hits the mark, you immediately take flight. You run hard with complete confidence that your forerunner will catch up with you and that the handover of the baton will be smooth.

Spiritually, we are to pass on the unchanging, incorruptible Word of God. This is not about repackaging the Gospel or coming up with a new message, for faith only comes by hearing the Word of God [Romans 10: 17]. Just like the relay, Paul said, 'My job was to plant the seed in your hearts, and Apollos watered, but God gave the *increase*. The ones who plant and the ones who water work as a team. They share the same purpose. They will be rewarded individually, according to their own hard work' [I Corinthians 3: 6-8]. The *Message* never changes.

To *increase* means to enlarge, to make greater, as in number, size, strength, or quality; augment; to grow, to expand and make abundance of. A correct transfer and proper increase will make it easier, quicker, more efficient, and better for the future generations to tap into the things of God and carry on with life. I believe God is looking for people who want more, see further, pass on the baton, build generationally, and desire to leave a lasting legacy. The Bible says, 'Enlarge the site of your tent to make room for more children. Stretch out the curtains of your dwellings. Do not spare them. Lengthen your tent ropes and make your pegs firm in the ground' [Isaiah 54: 2].

The power of continuity is born when we transfer generationally, gathering momentum which will result in exponential increase.

Striving for continuity, in fact, sharpens the Body of Christ for each new level. The Bible says, 'You shall file and sharpen them to penetrate and teach and impress them diligently upon the minds and hearts of your children' [Deuteronomy 6]. It also says that if the axe [our children or those we influence] is dull and its edge unsharpened, we must exert more strength, but skill will bring success [Ecclesiastes 10: 10]; but wisdom to sharpen the axe helps us succeed, with less effort. Let us therefore sharpen each generation, with our obvious aim being to get the generations to become sharper and more skilled. Jesus said, greater miracles than Him, shall the Church do [John 14: 12-14]. Ephesians 1 reminds us that we must run with purpose, clarity, significance, longevity, vision, and passion.

Man's primary habitat has always been God Himself [Psalm 91, Psalm 140: 13, Psalm 16: 11, Psalm 31: 20, & Psalm 9: 3]. Did you not hear what Paul said? 'In Him [God], we live and move and have our being? [Acts 17: 28]. Just as water is synonymous with fish, grasslands or woodlands with lions and the air with birds, Man lives in God. Without Him, Man will always suffocate, lose his way, and die [Genesis 3: 8 - 10]. Just look around you, the world is in total chaos. When Man prioritises the primary purpose—to please God, seeking first the Kingdom of God and His righteousness as well as growing in dominion mandate, our impact will be ceaseless. The Lord's plans will stand firm forever. The thoughts and intentions of His heart will under no circumstances, be shaken. They will last to all generations.

Where faithful men and women of God have walked, indelible imprints are evident. The Church will begin to affect schools, workplaces, neighbourhoods, villages, towns, cities, and nations. The nation that chooses our God as Lord will be blessed, for He will choose those people for His own inheritance. Generations with a desire to teach, to share, to transfer and to impart, must arise and initiate. This drive to pass the baton should be simulated by a pursuing generation with a complete yieldedness to God; humility [I Peter 5: 5], teachable hearts, a holy restlessness and determination to go further for genuine continuity to be birthed. The result will be an ever-maturing Church that easily taps into God, gathering momentum, having better acquaintances with the Holy Spirit, more intimacy, more faith, greater exploits, a superior harvest, and an aggregation of God moments, preparing the Bride for her Groom. Let us replicate people who have the Psalmist's attitude; those who will praise the Lord as long as they live. They will sing praises to God, even with their dying breath [Psalm 146: 2].

Let us, therefore, reproduce and stimulate generations of people who will trust and fully rely on God in every sphere of life, for eternity. The Bible says that "a generation goes, and a generation comes, but the earth remains forever" [Ecclesiastes 1: 4]. It also says, "One generation shall praise God's works to another and shall declare His mighty acts" [Psalm 145: 4]. For every generation that goes, another arises with more faith, more fervour, and greater works. It is unapologetic, taking territory, stirring the waters, creating ripples that build into wave after wave [tsunami] of faith-filled and completely sold-out people—a radical [rooted in Jesus Christ] breed who hold the standard. Those who will build a stone wall and refuse to bow or bend, people who refuse to be ductile or malleable to external pressures, those who will carry the same unchanging and unerring message through the passage of time. This wave upon wave of faith-filled people will begin to walk in a greater anointing; Generations who have resolved in themselves and are determined to be contagious, to stir up, impact, empower, release, and encourage subsequent generations.

In the Book of Jeremiah 1: 4 - 6, the words God spoke to Jeremiah, He is still repeating to men and women, even in our generation. 'Before you were born, I sanctified you; I set you apart or chose you for a special work.' Many still reply to Him, just as Jeremiah did, 'Lord, I'm too young; immature, unqualified, lack confidence or lack experience.' Ultimately, men and women in our day, then run away from God. They flee and end up outmaneuvered by the things of the world. They miss their primary purpose and end up tangled with the cares of life because of a lack of advice or guidance by those who 'know' God. Continuity is not just about us handing the baton only when we are about to retire or die. While we are full of vigour, let us also release and actively participate in the lives of our children, disciples, or those we influence. Let us not just tell them about our experiences; let us guide and instruct them on how to move forward. Let us give them the baton and keys.

Jesus instructed His twelve disciples to go into the entire world and preach the gospel [Matthew 28: 18 - 20] that is continuity. His instruction is a present continuous; that instruction still applies to us, the Church. The comfort to this instruction is found in Acts 1:8. We are not doing this alone; we have His Holy Spirit who gives us the ability to accomplish this task—power!

Jesus' Word is timeless, His presence is everlasting, His testimony is matchless, He was, He is, and He is to come. He split time and dispensations, B.C., Before Christ and A.D. He is present before the beginning in Genesis and still shows up all the way to Revelation. He is with us, He is in us, He is upon us, He is for us, He is working through us, and His legacy still lives on in our day. On this side of life, time is a valuable commodity. However, when you depart from this life and step into eternity, time does not exist and has no meaning. This is regardless of where you end up, Heaven or Hell. Here is why time is so valuable; seconds make up minutes, minutes make up hours, hours make up days, days into weeks and weeks into months. Months and years make up seasons.

The Psalmist asks God to teach us to number our days that we may get a heart of wisdom [90: 12]. In Ephesians 5: 15 - 16, Paul pleads with the Church to look carefully how She walks, not as unwise but as wise, making the best use of time, because the days ahead are evil. When I was a young boy, I often went to our rural home and spent many times herding cattle with others. I became a good student of seasons and time. I could tell the time of day just by looking at the position of the sun. I also knew the times and when we were transitioning between seasons just by looking at nature: the trees, the shrubs as well as the scarcity of wild animals. As Christians, let us understand our spiritual seasons and time. Like the sons of Issachar, we need to know the times [I Chronicles 12: 32]. Jesus' words still echo today, a present continuous, directed at you and me. Paul caught this, and as I read, in the periphery of some of his letters to the Church, with teachings, corrections, rebukes, and revelations, Paul alludes to continuity.

For example, Paul agonised for the Churches in Galatia [Galatians 4: 19]: "My little children, of whom I travail in birth again until *Christ be formed in you."* Paul's drive was for continuity. On another occasion, Paul urged the Church at Corinth to imitate him as he imitated Christ [I Corinthians 4: 16 & 11: 1]. Paul's reason was continuity. To the saints in Philippi [Philippians 4: 9], he said, "Whatever you have *learned* and *received* and *heard* from me *and seen in me,* put these things into *practice.* And the God of peace will be with you." Paul was pushing for continuity. In his letter to Timothy, Paul is unequivocally clear that the things that Timothy has heard from him among many witnesses for Timothy to *entrust these to faithful men* who will be competent to *teach others also* [II Timothy 2: 2].

Let me enlighten you about what it means to be *entrusted* with something. Firstly, if you cannot be trusted, no one will entrust anything to you. A Trustee is a person or legal entity given control or powers of administration of property in trust, with a legal obligation to administer it solely for the purposes specified. To be appointed a Trustee is an enormous responsibility. In the fiduciary industry, Trustees are vetted. You must be qualified and demonstrate competency. Trustees are entrusted with a wide range of assets, from significant cash deposits, investments, stocks and shares, intellectual property, to residential and commercial properties. Paul was saying to Timothy, handle the things of God with due reverence and awe, then vet and identify, teach, train, empower, pass on, and release other faithful, competent men for the sake of continuity. Identifying is not just about people's function; it is also about instilling Godly character, discipline, and authenticity [II Timothy 2: 15]—to the glory of God.

Earth shall be filled with the glory of the Lord as the waters cover the sea [Habakkuk 2: 14] because the Church is walking in a greater anointing. As recorded by Ezekiel [47: 1 - 5], over time and through the generations, our depth, experience, and knowledge and love of God will increase and ooze out of the Bride. Just like the oil that flowed down on Jehu [II Kings 9: 4 - 12] or the many oils applied on Esther by the Custodian [Esther 2: 12], and confirmed in Psalm 133: 2, the anointing oil will be tangibly evident. We are supposed to be like rivers [John 7: 38], continuously flowing with fresh water, feeding other tributaries [blessing the generations] for eternity, and not supposed to be swamps [one generation wonders or superstars], whose water loses freshness over time, becomes a stench, and dries with no traces of ever having existed.

In our day, let us refuse to be like the Pharisees and Sadducees [Matthew 23: 1 - 2]. For the 400 years between the prophet Malachi and the writings of Matthew, they initiated and handed down practices and rituals, which hardened man's heart from hearing God. Jesus said to them, "You have a fine way of rejecting the commandment of God in order to establish your tradition, making void the word of God by your tradition that you have handed down." [Mark 7: 9 - 13 paraphrased]. God was never silent. Man's heart grew dark and cold, authentic continuity and fellowship was broken, and God started again. He raised John the Baptist. John rightly called the scribes and pharisees a generation of vipers—snakes [Matthew 3: 7]. Jesus encouraged the people to listen and respect to the scribes and pharisees, but not to live like them [Matthew 23]. The shocking reality is that there is a parallel, albeit very subtle, to some of our modern-day executive apostles, executive pastors, executive prophets, and executive evangelists, who have walked into extreme and potentially toxic territories, replacing Christ with their platforms of money, aeroplanes, television networks, and multiple story buildings ["these things"]. Jesus calls these people blind guides and warns us to stay clear of them [Matthew 23: 24 - 25 & 15: 14]. Isaiah the prophet called them shepherds who have no understanding. He then elaborates at how depraved their hearts are [Isaiah 56: 11 - 12]. I am not against owning houses and land but let us not make flaunting "these things" be the principal thing.

Like never before, the Church—a city on a hill, the light of the world [Matthew 5: 14] needs to shine brighter, lead the way, and set the pace. The Church needs to move at God's speed. The Church needs to remain relevant and not become a relic, to be the pillar, the pulse, and the heartbeat of every society. It is when we responsibly demonstrate God's love and faithfulness, teach skills, transfer ability, impart wisdom, share our experiences, successes and failures or errors and mistakes and then finally emphasise on character above gifts that we will see godly Stewards who will transfer faith, finances, relationships, leadership, and life experiences to coming generations.

Our lives must be like an open book, not one with dead letters but living epistles for all to see and learn.

The reality is that not everyone is called to the five-fold ministry [Ephesians 4: 11]. Most are saints [Ephesians 4: 12] and a royal priesthood [I Peter 2: 9]. Some people will network; others will be gardeners, and others will be politicians, doctors, or businesspeople. Our primary purpose is to please God [Colossians 3: 23], not to place servitude on a pedestal, not to idolise or pervert gifts, and not to measure oneself by role but to understand that our identity is found in God and not in things or positions. We each need to run our race, with such conviction, passion, and aggression, always to pass on the mantle to someone else. Let me be clear, we are not attempting to make the name of Jesus famous. Jesus is not a brand; Coca cola, Denim and Rolex are famous brands and are widely recognised, but it does not mean everyone likes them. Fame is always subject to preference and interpretation. These famous brands are optional. Some prefer Pepsi over Coca Cola while others prefer Wrangler over Denim, and yet others prefer Audemars Piguet over Rolex watches. Jesus Christ is a necessity; He is not an option, just as you and I have no choice in the matter in choosing Ozone [O_3] over Oxygen [O_2], or Hydrogen Peroxide [H_2O_2] over water [H_2O], for survival. Ozone molecule contains three oxygen atoms, instead of two oxygen atoms which make up atmospheric oxygen which is necessary for survival. A Hydrogen Peroxide molecule contains two Hydrogen atoms and two Oxygen atoms, which do not make a substitute of water, whose molecule is made up of two Hydrogen atoms and one oxygen atom. Ozone and Hydrogen Peroxide, whilst they closely look like atmospheric oxygen and water respectively, they are not the real deal. An imitation of the real substance will not do. Jesus is a need and not just a want, to every human being. Our aim must be to 'arrest' people from blindly walking under deception to a lost eternity, bring them to a loving relationship with Jesus Christ, and fulfil our call to pursue God [Philippians 3:12-14]. The blows we strike must not be aimless [I Corinthians 9: 25 - 27]. We must accomplish and fulfil our mission in order for those who follow behind to do it even better.

In Paul's letter to Timothy [II Timothy 2: 2], we see that they are participants as well as spectators [witnesses]. The only people who are afforded the privilege of being spectators are those we find in Hebrews 12, and believe me, they are not silent but are spurring us on. Paul reminds Timothy of Witnesses. To witness is to watch, to be a spectator. Participants throw caution to the wind and enter the race, and they realise that God's reputation must be upheld, regardless of cost. Our journey here on earth is not a sprint. It is like a long-distance race, and it requires longevity, stamina, endurance, patience, toughness, and aggression. The racetrack must have our footprints, marks to show that we came and left something permanent, marks for others to follow, marks of inspiration, marks of encouragement and marks to challenge and stir. For generations, our mark must be seen, felt, and heard—we must leave a lasting legacy, to the glory of God. We need to learn and know when to power, when to sprint, when to coast [to allow the Holy Spirit to be in charge], and when to allow momentum to take us to the finish line—we need to finish strong. Let us not talk a good talk; let us walk the talk. Let us not try and look the part; let us be the real Church. As the prophet of old Joel said, rend your hearts, not just your garments. Come back to God, your God. And here's why: God is kind and merciful. He takes a deep breath, puts up with a lot, this most patient God, extravagant in love, always ready to cancel catastrophe. Who knows? Maybe he'll do it now; maybe he'll turn around and show pity. Maybe, when all's said and done, there'll be blessings full and robust for your God! [Joel 2: 13 MSG].

Paul writes to Titus and paints a picture of old and young, the wise and youth, to blend and ensure continuity:

Titus 2: 1 - 9 (ESV)
"But as for you, teach what accords with sound doctrine. Older men are to be sober minded, dignified, self-controlled, sound in faith, in

love, and in steadfastness. Older women likewise are to be reverent in behaviour, not slanderers or slaves to much wine. They are to teach what is good, and so train the young women to love their husbands and children, to be self-controlled, pure, working at home, kind, and submissive to their own husbands, that the word of God may not be reviled. Likewise, urge the younger men to be self-controlled. Show yourself in all respects to be a model of good works, and in your teaching show integrity, dignity, and sound speech that cannot be condemned, so that an opponent may be put to shame, having nothing evil to say about us."

Continuity is birthed when we appreciate and embrace every moment of life. This will result in an aggregation or quantum of moments, giving rise to perpetual momentum. Because of momentum, subsequent generations will birth enduring, experienced, uncompromising generations. The end result will be an ever-maturing Church, which confidently occupies and eats the good of the land, as She waits expectantly for Christ's return.

As we peer into the heart of God, we see how the Father commends Jesus and instructs us [the world] to listen to Him. "This is my beloved Son in whom I am well pleased." [Matthew 3: 17]. The Father is informing us that Jesus' actions and words are very God. The Father has passed on authority to his Son, to carry out His works here on earth, which is continuity. We also see how Jesus fully embraced and honoured everything of the Father, even unto death. Be determined and make these words be yours for your children and those you will influence. "But as for me and my household, we will serve the Lord." [Joshua 24: 15b].

In Isaiah 55: 8 - 9, God says to Man, "For My thoughts are not your thoughts, nor are your ways My ways, for as the heavens are higher than the earth, so are My ways higher than your ways, and My thoughts than your thoughts." If we would only desire to align and recalibrate our lives to God's ways, we would turn this world upside down. The beginning of this journey is in our mind, which will force our thoughts into actions and habits. The Bible says, 'Let this mind be in you, which was also in Christ Jesus [Philippians 2: 5]. Why? Because you have the mind of Christ' [I Corinthians 2: 16].

Ask yourself these questions: Who is cut from the same cloth as you? Who are you influencing, so that what you have is evident in the coming generations?

Moses led Joshua [Israel] out of Egypt [bondage and slavery] and into the wilderness—that was the next level! Joshua led the nation of Israel into the promise land but was supposed to have influenced another! Caleb [Joshua 14] influenced a younger generation; at 85 years old he maintained his fervour, his vigour, and his uncompromising faith in God [verse 10 - 14]. David saw the return of the ark of covenant back to Israel and inspired his son Solomon to build the temple [House of God]—greater works and greater results! Jesus, the Christ did great exploits, but emphasised that we would do even greater than He did [John 14: 12]—increase in the anointing! Every father, father figure, mother, or mentor is supposed to want more from their children. I am yet to meet a parent who wants to hog onto power, be the only one who supposedly knows it all and has the franchise to the anointing. If you have met such people, they have missed God's plan. Moses understood God, that he praised Him saying, "Lord, You have been our dwelling place [our refuge, our sanctuary, our stability] in all generations." [Psalm 90: 1]. God is God throughout all generations. Moses loved the presence of God, that he would not move without Him [Exodus 33: 15]. Moses' example and practice were passed on and fully embraced by Joshua too; when everyone else moved away, Joshua stayed at the tent because of his love for God's presence.

Dwelling place speaks of permanence, not temporary or one-off; it is further emphasised by the Psalmist 91: 1 - 2. This is what Ephesians 3: 17 means, and what Jesus meant when He said, "My Father and I will make you our dwelling place" [John 14: 23]. He further prayed, "I in them [the Church] and You in me [John 17: 23]. Paul asked the Church, "Do you not know that your bodies are temples of God?" [I Corinthians 3: 16]. He then reminds the Church again that we are temples of God [II Corinthians 6: 16]. When God's presence, authority, His explosiveness, and expressiveness collide with true humility and yieldedness, it births initiators that step up and step out. When you and I glean from our predecessors, we will embrace both, a physical and a spiritual inheritance.

Whenever focus moves from kingdom to self, we negate, nullify, and cancel the ability to propagate, perpetuate, or establish anything that is eternal. We must take our eyes from self to kingdom, family, and team. Building your own name—a self-made man will yield temporal results. Regardless of the right things you may say, people who learn from you will catch and become the person you are. You will replicate yourself in the next generation. I am convinced that your beginning will always be humble [Job 8: 7] regardless of what you begin with. I say this, measured against what the latter or future will be. What begins like drops or a trickle of water will build into a tsunami, what begins as a spark or flame will erupt into a forceful and unstoppable volcano, and what begins as a tune will become an endless symphony. Remember, what began in a lonely stable in Bethlehem has spread across the earth, and Jesus Christ of Nazareth our Lord and Saviour is praised the world over. It is no mistake that Haggai prophesied and said, the glory of the latter house, shall exceed the glory of the former [Haggai 2: 9]. When we catch this, we will dedicate our time, our talents and treasure to God and become participants, catalysts, and initiators of 'forever'.

Some who have gone before us have completely misrepresented the Kingdom. They have done Jesus Christ a disservice and treated His finished work on the cross with contempt. They treated Him as common and elevated their own priorities and interests ahead of the Kingdom. Some gained earthly riches, built their names, and thought they had arrived. Others not only got intimidated, but they cowered and hid and never resurrected from their condition. As a result, ideas, strategies, and phenomenal concepts were never tapped. Everything was buried with them, making some graveyards places of completely unaccomplished, unrealised, and unfulfilled potential. They are also places of both sorrow and pain. We need to change this mindset. Future generations of those buried must be people who fulfil the number of days set before them, people who achieved their purpose, followed the leading of the Holy Spirit and answered the call of God every step of the way. Generations who did not die prematurely but emptied everything. Their accomplishments will be well noted on earth, and resound in Heaven, as their names are added to Hebrews 11. Yes, we will miss their physical presence here on earth but rejoice at their exemplary lives.

Perhaps you may be like me, exposed to corporate meetings and gatherings, social club functions and even school events, and heard words like 'continuity, progression, and succession,' being banded around? These are shrewd people in the world. It is however quite unfortunate that once you get the same people saved and they come into the kingdom of God, these words are suddenly lost. It is as though people become self-centred, completely lose focus on others, and only look forward to dying and going to Heaven. We need to realise that God has a phenomenal plan for each of us, and that plan includes others. He wants eternity birthed through us! We must each run our races and remain in our lanes, affecting and influencing others along. We need to see the Church become well-oiled and come to maturity.

As you read further, flow with me, let me take you on a ride that prepares you to move into more with God. Let the anointing that is already upon you flow down your head, right down to those who follow behind you, let it be so evident that those around get caught up in the same anointing in an even mightier way than you, and then allow the fire of the Holy Spirit to set you alight. Glow warm, be infectious, be the light, and refuse to go unheard. Let us put away the lack of continuity. Today we nail the gravestone of ignorance, lethargy, timidity, fear of man, religion, spiritual coma—and say, "Never again!"

The reason the Bible says that we are written epistles [II Corinthians 3: 1 - 3] is all about continuity. When people see you, they are literally reading God's word and will encounter Him through you! We arise and take full responsibility to fix this matter. Let's be people of integrity, so that God upholds us and sets us in His presence forever [Psalm 41: 12]. We in turn will "birth" people just like us [I John 2: 13 – 14].

THE HERITAGE OF FAITH

Isaiah 59: 21 (KJV)

As for me, this is my covenant with them, saith the Lord, my spirit that is upon thee, and my words which I have put in thy mouth, shall not depart from thy mouth, nor out of the mouth of thy seed, nor out of the mouth of thy seed's seed, saith the Lord, from henceforth and forever.

According to Isaiah, the Holy Spirit in us, and the word of God in us must go from generation to generation. Here is a statement made by Jesus, concerning the Holy Spirit and forever or eternity, which the New Testament Believer needs to let sink into the inner man. Jesus spoke these words to the Samaritan woman, "but anyone who drinks of the water [Holy Spirit] I will give will never be thirsty again. The water [Holy Spirit] that I will give will become in him a spring of water welling up forever" [John 4: 14]

You see, faith must always come first. Why, you ask? The answer is simple, without faith it is impossible to please God [Hebrews 11: 6]. In order for any generation to navigate and make it through life, it is faith that will hold them together. Faith is the biggest thing you can give anyone, so that when you are long gone, they have the fortitude to withstand whatever is thrown their way. You can give anyone your precious materials [cars, houses, and businesses], but how will they walk through life, if they lose all the material possessions? What will benefit the person if they are destined for Hell? [Mark 8: 36].

Have you ever wondered why the Bible has genealogies or lineages recorded in it? Bible Scholars inform us that there are no less than twenty lineages that are documented in the Holy Bible. Lineages highlight continuity. Matthew Chapter 1 records Abraham's lineage. Where continuity is concerned, Abraham is by far heads and shoulders above everyone else. This is also re-iterated in Hebrews 11. Being the father of faith, all disciples of Jesus Christ are descendants of Abraham. Abraham initiated a heritage that cascaded, all the way to Jesus Christ, and still endures in our day all the way to eternity. Someone may think that all the people in Abraham's lineage were priestly - on the contrary, some were converted thieves, prostitutes, murderers, carpenters, kings, warriors; the list is long. These people looked beyond their circumstances and situation. Their common denominator was their love and faith in God. You and I live in the best time of human history, we are temples of God, and we are led by the Holy Spirit. I came across Ezra 2 where several lineages are listed. Amid those that came from captivity, were several people who did not know their genealogy or lineage [read verse 58 - 63]. Their identity or qualification for entry into the acceptable lineage had to be determined by a priest who would consult with the Urim and Thummim.

In our day, I thank God that Jesus Christ is our qualification. Once you have Him, you qualify. Each of us has a lineage. My question to you is: Do you have a heritage of faith? How many in your lineage were disciples of Jesus Christ? If you are a first-generation Christian in your lineage, then you are a pioneer. You are like Abraham, go for it! Initiate! The fact that you are reading this book probably means that you are born again. Someone introduced you and invited you into a loving relationship with our Heavenly Father, through His son Jesus Christ. You therefore have a heritage of faith. Can you also imagine what it would have been like to have been a Moses, given up by your parents? Perhaps being a David, whose parents and brothers saw you as a nobody? Both were used by God as can you. They triggered a ripple effect. My challenge to each of us is to be like Jabez in I Chronicles. You may not know your heritage or lineage, but that should not stop you from crying out to God. Why you ask? I John 4: 4 is the answer, "you are of God." Each of us must become initiators of a God-fearing lineage—may He give you more influence and expand your territory until Jesus returns.

Speaking of our Lord Jesus Christ, Isaiah also prophesied that His ever expanding, peaceful government will never end. He will rule with fairness and justice from the throne of His ancestor David [Isaiah 9: 7]. When Jesus arrived on the scene and asked the question in Luke 18: 8b, He was clearly looking into the future and had a good reason for asking. It is not a coincidence or mistake. In one of His last instructions, Jesus said, "Therefore, go and make disciples of all nations, baptising them in the name of the Father, and of the Son, and of the Holy Spirit." Jesus was delegating, transferring, and conferring his authority to his disciples [the Church, that is us!]—continuity was on His mind.

Jesus was setting the ball in motion, and that ball is now in our court. Faith must be transferred from generation to generation. The Holy Spirit and God's Word in us must never dissipate and must not die with us. We are to overflow. We must pour out into our children, spiritual sons, and those we influence, so that they, in turn, pour into others. Consequently, the cycle of forever is created. That is why Isaiah [in Chapter 59: 21] said *forever*, which means without end. In Deuteronomy 29: 29, Moses said, "The secret things belong to the Lord our God, but the revealed things belong to us and to our children forever, that we may do all the words of this law."

In Luke 1, God identified Elizabeth [a mature lady] and Mary [a young lady] who, coincidentally, were relatives and ended up being vessels that carried the greatest prophet, and the only begotten Son of God, respectively. In an era, where the voice of the Lord was rare, these two women must have had something that caught God's attention. Clearly, they were passionate about God and likely conferred and spurred each other on. They often visited each other and shared their hearts. The Bible says, the eyes of the Lord run to-and-fro throughout all the earth to show Himself strong on behalf of them whose *heart* is loyal to Him [II Chronicles 16: 9]. The Word of God says, "Above all else, guard your *heart*, for everything you do flows from it" [Proverbs 4: 23]. We are also reminded to "Draw nigh to God, and He will draw nigh to you." Cleanse your hands, ye sinners; and purify your hearts, ye double minded" [James 4: 8].

Isaiah prophesied, and Jesus spoke the words, "These people honour Me with their lips, but their hearts are far from Me" [Isaiah 29: 13 & Matthew 15: 8]. Furthermore, God says this of Man's heart, "O that there was such a heart in them, that they would fear Me, and keep all My commandments always, that it might be well with them, and with their children forever!" [Deuteronomy 5: 29]. Like begets like, and inwardly, Elizabeth and Mary looked like each other [they both pursued God!], and God sought and found them.

Some people have received Jesus Christ as their Saviour but not as Lord [the one who is sovereign]. The truth is that the responsibility has always been in our hands; it has always been the condition of the heart of man, as to whether we draw near to Him or not. God is never silent; if one generation gets it wrong, the repercussions can be devastating. Here is a lesson for us; since calvary, God has done all He can to keep this relationship with Man alive—now let's pass on the faith message to others. Let us therefore lead people to Jesus: our homes, our communities, our places of influence and work environments with skilful hands and integrity of heart [Psalms 78: 72].

The story of King Herod [who represents God's chosen people], and the wise men [Men from East], fascinates me. The Jews [Herod] had written evidence before the birth of Jesus. Holy men of old had prophesied the coming of the King. Numerous prophecies were made by the prophets including, Micah [Chapter 5: 2] and Isaiah [Chapter 9: 6 - 7], and yet the Jews seemed to be in a spiritual coma upon Jesus' arrival. On the other hand, the wise men who came from the East [Matthew 2] had obviously been on the lookout for the star, for One who was to be born King of the Jews. We are not told much about these men; exactly who they were is a mystery. I am not going to speculate or debate. The Bible is explicit that these were God-fearing men. Here are a couple of thoughts and questions for you to chew on. These men knew God; they presented gifts of gold, frankincense, and myrrh to the King [Jesus Christ]. All were presents of symbolic

His kingship, His divinity, and His death [Matthew 2: 11]. These men were subsequently divinely warned [Matthew 2: 12] not to go back to Herod—and they obeyed God. A thought: Why would they have travelled that distance to pay homage to Jesus if they did not understand that this birth was a significant moment for the Jews and all of humanity? The wise men travelled from a distant land and into Jewish territory, to pay homage to the Christ, the Messiah, and King of the Jews.

Meanwhile, the Jews ignorantly lived from day to day, like every other day. The Jews had not interpreted the times, and the fact that something very significant was taking place. The birth of Jesus was a day when the *Chronos* of Man and the *Kyros* of God collided. It was the moment God came in the flesh to live with Man. Heaven knew it and celebrated; Hell pondered its next move, and Earth's timeline was about to change [B.C to A.D]. All of humanity could now acquaint themselves with God, the creator of Heaven and Earth, as Father and friend. It is clear to me that Herod knew very little of his Jewish lineage. Had he known how his forefather, King Josiah, had reacted when God's Word was discovered [read II Kings 22], Herod would have turned to the Messiah. We observe from these accounts that archiving historic events and important records and then forgetting about them is not new.

The Book of the Prophet was eventually pulled out of the archives at the request of King Herod [Matthew 2: 4 - 5]. It had probably been gathering dust, when the birth of the Messiah was read and confirmed by the Chief Priest and scribes. It is possible that the Books of Prophets, which were highly valued, sought after, and observed in one generation were now in some closet and not being studied, in another generation. The information about the coming Messiah King would have, down through the generations, been long forgotten, never opened, and probably viewed as something ancient. No king would have wanted to know that his throne and rulership were temporary. Generations would have passed on fear and timidity to each subsequent generation. This new generation did not discern or understand God's seasons and timing. The Bible says, 'He changes times and seasons; he removes kings and sets up kings; he gives wisdom to the wise and knowledge to those who have understanding' [Daniel 2: 21].

While the Jews who should have known of the coming Messiah, archived, and forgot the documented evidence between generations, somewhere in a country in the East, God inspired other unknown men about a future King of the Jews, whose government knows no end. To the men in the East, the sign of the Messiah's arrival would be announced by His star. I am convinced that the word of the coming King of the Jews was not given overnight but would have been an equally enduring word, being passed from generation to generation. In this country in the East, through generations, men would have been waiting with excitement and anticipation. Careful planning would have been made and decided concerning presents worthy of the King of kings.

Let us fast-forward years later when the boy Jesus was now a man and His ministry impacting Israel and the world. What became of the descendants or younger generations of the men from the East who had heralded the King of kings? Did these men pass the message to their descendants to continue visiting the King?

In studying the Bible, too, I see a repeated failure by Man to pass on the mantle to the next generation. Often, there is a common theme of successes by one generation and the fall of the next. We witness one bumper harvest, a mighty move of God, a transformation of lives, and then, a succession of spiritual decadents and spiritual droughts. Thank God for His enduring love, His tender mercy, and His relentless persistence towards humanity. God consistently restores and begins all over again. Observe from the Bible:

- There is Moses, Joshua, and **someone was supposed to come after Joshua**.

- There is Elijah, Elisha, and **someone was expected to come after Elisha.**
- There is David, Solomon, and **someone was supposed to come after Solomon.**
- There is Jesus, Peter, and **someone who is expected to come after Peter.**
- There is Jesus, Lois, Eunice, Timothy, **and someone who is expected to come after Timothy.**
- There is Jesus, Philip, his four prophetess daughters, **and someone who is expected to come after them.**

At every plunge of man, God regenerates, reconstructs, re-engineers, revives, and restores His purpose and plan through a willing and obedient individual. Often, in English, the word **RE**, concisely means, "To start again." For example, revivals are supernatural and are a move of God. The sad truth, however, is that revivals are a resuscitation of man; it is the bringing back of Man to God consciousness. Revivals cause humans to **rediscover** the truth and their fellowship with God. Simply put, it is something that was known, which somewhere along the line got lost and is eventually found again. I am not against revivals—I just came to tell you that this was not part of God's original plan, and those of us who know Him must ensure those around us know Him too.

When I think of faith and continuity in the New Testament, I believe that Lois, Timothy's grandmother, stands out. You see, whatever Grandma Lois carried, she passed it on to her daughter Eunice, who in turn passed it on to Timothy. I believe Timothy moved and walked in greater levels of faith than those before him. I believe that Lois and Eunice only had a glimpse of the things which eventually became tangible for Timothy. Timothy was operating in a greater anointing. The two women had the anointing of God, as well as a wealth of experience, and this made it easier for Timothy to use their peaks as his foundation. Paul became Timothy's spiritual father. The faith that was in both women convinced Paul that the same faith was in

Timothy too. So, it came as no surprise to Paul when he met Timothy and took him under his wing. Paul said this to Timothy:

II Timothy 1: 5 (KJV)
*When I call to remembrance the **unfeigned faith that is in thee**, which dwelt **first** in thy **grandmother Lois and thy mother Eunice**, I am persuaded that it is in thee also.*

In Timothy's case, the Bible tells us that his father was Greek, Acts 16. We are not given much more information about his father. What we do know is that Timothy's faith heritage came from his mother's side of the family. Timothy did not allow a Greek background or tradition to define or mould him. The Bible says that his mother was Jewish, and she became convinced that Jesus is the Messiah. In turn, she told her son, resulting in Timothy's yielded obedience to Jesus [Acts 16: 1]. We must pass on this faith message; this baton must be passed on for the relay to continue without a disqualification or dropping of the baton. Notice however, that though parents initiate, this relationship is reciprocal. There is a level of responsibility placed upon the children as well. Failure by the children is not always a reflection of the parent. Children must be teachable; they must remain humble and wait their turn, when released by their parents. The Bible says:

Ephesians 6:1- 3 (Amplified Bible)
*"Children, obey your parents in the Lord [as his representatives], for this is right. Honour [esteem and value as precious] your father and mother—this is the first commandment with a promise—**that all may be well with you and that you may live long on the earth."***

In II Kings 2, the story of Elijah and Elisha also clearly illustrates how any child should be with their parent—father, father figure, mother, mentor, or spiritual parent. Elijah saw that Elisha desired something. Elisha stuck it out; in verse 13, Elisha took up the mantle of Elijah that fell as the chariots of fire took Elijah. Elisha received the baton and took the ministry further. A failure to influence and teach the next generation in the things of

God will result in weak genes being passed on within the Body of Christ. This will lead to a form of godliness, decay in the moral fabric of our society, and ultimately, death. Let me warn you, so that you do not become like Eli, or a son of Eli.

We need to be people who carry the name and recognise the significance, the power, and the authority.

[Read Samuel 2]

There are three things I would like to highlight from the above chapter:

- An Old Testament priest generally spoke God's ordinances and commands; Eli stood in this office.
- The priests were of Aaron's lineage and ministered before God. The priests presented items to God that were to be sacrificed, and these priests represented the people. Hophni and Phineas, the sons of the prophet Eli, were priests from the lineage of Aaron.
- Eli and his sons were supposed to symbolise unity, strength, and continuity.

Looking closely at the meanings of the names of the three main characters, reveals some clues at God's expectations:

- Eli - Ancient word for God
- Hophni - Fighter
- Phineas - Oracle

God loved Eli so much that He gave him His name. When people called him by name, Eli was supposed to remember God. Hophni, the fighter, was meant to fight, defending the things of God. He was to be God's hands and feet. He was not supposed to settle for anything less, and through him, God was to be magnified. Phineas was to speak the word of God. He was to be God's spokesman and mouthpiece. The words leaving his mouth were supposed to be tender in love, soothing in healing and sharp in correction. Instead, here is what the Bible says:

I Samuel 2: 1a (NKJV)
*Now the sons of Eli were sons of **Belial***

Belial is a Hebrew word which means corrupt, perverted, and worthless scoundrels. Can you imagine priests, and sons with such beautiful names, being called Belial? How do we reconcile this? It is evident from the Bible that the mistakes began with their father, Eli. He was the problem, and it filtered into his seed. Eli failed as a father and failed to pass on the baton to the next generation. He preferred his sons ahead of God. In the New Living Translation, I Samuel 2:29b, God said to Eli, 'Why do you honour your children more than me - for you, and they have become fat from the best offerings of my people!' Eli did not teach his sons to walk with God; he loved them so much that he admired them. He idolised them and placed them on the pedestal of his heart. He must have thought that, by chance, they would eventually understand and receive revelation of who God was - often a clear mistake that we see regularly, even in our day. When the sons took the best offering, I am convinced that they shared with their father. It is recorded in I Samuel 4:18 that in stature, Eli was a massive man.

Eli stopped hearing from God first. Proverbs 4:23 says to keep your heart with all vigilance, for from it flows the spring of life. We can externally wear the same style of clothes as our mentors or spiritual fathers, preach with charisma, and still be way off the mark. The Bible says, 'Rend your hearts and not your garments' [Joel 2: 13]. Remember, the internal is more important. Eli, God's priest, spoke and dressed like the priest, but his heart was far from God. If we fail to hear from God, it is not that He has stopped talking but merely that we have stopped listening. In Eli's case, God eventually used ordinary people, the equivalent of members of the public, to speak to the man of God, who now loosely carried the name of God. Is this not astonishing?

I Samuel 2: 24 (NLT)
Eli heard from the people what his sons were doing.

In I Samuel 2: 25a, the Bible shows that Eli's judgment then became clouded. Had he picked the baton, run with it smoothly afterwards, he would have learned previous lessons from his forefather Moses. Moses had continuously interceded for backslidden Israel, and yet Eli was unable to do so for his sons. As if to add insult to injury, Eli's place of authority, as God's delegated head of the family, was undermined by his sons. The Bible says, "But Eli's sons would not listen to their father, for the Lord was already planning to put them to death" [I Samuel 2: 25b]. The Kingdom is a Father-and-Son affair, and we need to replicate the same here on earth. This relationship is reciprocal; sons [children] must relate to their parents. In a relay, when one person drops the baton, the whole team is automatically disqualified, regardless of how hard one member ran. Whether he or she was in the lead or not, dropping the baton is as good as never having even started the relay. Spiritually speaking, dropping the baton can result in premature death.

What I found to be of concern is that Hophni and Phineas apparently did not know God. They did not follow the protocol clearly laid out to honour and please God. During the sacrifice, it reads, 'Now the sons of Eli were scoundrels who had no respect for the Lord' [I Samuel 2: 12]. They loved titles but did not hold the qualities of the office. Hophni and Phineas clearly had a form of godliness but denied the real power of God. They are likened to those who liked walking in the marketplace and being called 'priest!' In the New Testament days, Jesus would have described Hophni and Phineas this way. 'All of their works were done to be seen by men. They made their phylacteries broad and enlarged the borders of their garments. They loved the uppermost rooms at feasts, the chief seats in the synagogues, greetings in the markets, and to be called "Rabbi, Rabbi"' [Matthew 23: 5 - 7].

When you pull away from God, who is the very environment in which you were created to function, in desperation, you end up doing strange things. Hophni and Phineas enjoyed the pleasures of this world and committed sexual sins. Now, Eli was timeworn: He heard everything his sons did to Israel and how they lay with the women who assembled at the door of the tabernacle of meeting [I Samuel 2: 22]. Even though he had a wife at home (the Bible says he had a spouse), this was not enough for Phineas [I Samuel 4: 19]. It is not clear whether Hophni had a wife. What we do know is that they both had no excuse for their actions. As a result of this, the line of Eli ended, and God had to re-engineer another plan [God raised Samuel] for the sake of continuity. However, just like his mentor and male example before him, Samuel's sons, Joel and Abijah also did not walk in the ways of their father. They took bribes and perverted justice. Continuity ceased.

Now, compare Eli with the Deacon, Philip [Acts 6: 5], who raised four sexually pure daughters, who prophesied [Acts 21: 9]. It is evident to me that Philip governed his home well [I Timothy 3: 12 & 13] He was hospitable, too, as his house seemed to enjoy frequent visits from the Church. It is not a coincidence that his daughters turned out the way they did. They prophesied, and it is likely that they learned from other more experienced prophets such as Agabus the prophet who in Philip's house prophesied over Paul [Acts 21: 11]. Do you have the genes of God? Do you demonstrate these in your household, or are you a Sunday, Easter, or Christmas only Christian? God is challenging us to fix our homes, sphere of influence, our community, and places of work ahead of reaching the nations [Acts 1: 8]. If we take these small steps, God will give us the nations.

Just as real as the Godhead is for the saints who have graduated to glory, the same reality and faith [confidence, trust] in God by us [His Church] must be seen on earth. It must be a tangible reality of God. This trust level must grow and bubble over through each generation as we give a reason for the hope and faith that is in us to the next generation [I Peter 3: 15]. As each generation passes by, the baton passed should result in greater faith. A lasting legacy of faith must never be taken lightly. Faith should never decrease with time; instead, there must be an increment of the level of faith from father to son to grandson, great grandson, and the coming generations.

One of my favourite chapters in the Bible is Nehemiah 8. We can learn a lot from both Nehemiah and Ezra. Good fathers must be like Ezra the priest; they read God's word [morning until midday], breathe God's word, live God's word, and patiently teach the young men and women, until they get it. Good fathers persist until the young generation get it and say, "Amen, Amen!" The young generation approaches the old who are initiators, and these initiators oblige resulting in faith being transferred.

My recent observations are that sons are after authenticity. We should not wonder why some sons do not have a higher level of faith or have no faith at all. Sometimes, it is because we are public superstars, Sunday meeting and conference superstars, yet we are full of dead men's bones [Matthew 23: 27], whitewashed graves. It is because in the privacy of our homes, we never pray, never teach, never love, and never lead by example. It is time for fathers, father figures, mothers, spiritual parents, and mentors to get real with God. Ponder and meditate on this from the writer of the Book of Hebrews. In concluding, commending, and bestowing all the plaudits on the heroes of faith in Chapter 11, the author explains that God has better, and greater things planned for us. He implies that we, the new generation, are coming to maturity; therefore, as we have received Christ Jesus the Lord, so walk in Him, rooted, and built up in Him, and established in the faith, just as you were taught, abounding in thanksgiving.

Hebrews 11:39 - 40 (AMP)
And all of these, though they won divine approval by [means of] their faith, did not receive the fulfilment of what was promised, because God had us in mind and had something better and greater in view for us so that they [these heroes and heroines of faith] should not come to perfection apart from us [before we could join them].

AGGREGATION OF EXPERIENCES

Job 8: 8 - 10 (NLT)
Just ask the previous generation. Pay attention to the experience of our ancestors, for we were born but yesterday, and knowing nothing, our days on earth are as fleeting as a shadow. But those who came before us will teach you. They will teach you the wisdom of old.

Deuteronomy 4: 9 (with my emphasis)
Only take care and keep your soul diligently, lest you forget the things that your eyes have seen [you have experienced], and lest they depart from your heart all the days of your life. Make them known to your children and your children's children.

Psalm 127: 4 - 5 (AMP)
As arrows are in the hand of a warrior, so are the children of one's youth. Happy, blessed, and fortunate is the man whose quiver is filled with them! They will not be put to shame when they speak with their adversaries [in gatherings] at the [city's] gate.

Let me start by saying that I do not want us to overrate experience, just the same way we must never overrate qualification. In fact, when you are born again and are Spirit-filled, God lives in you. Although you may lack any form of experience, the One who lives in you has all the experience. The Ancient of Days lives in you. Since before time immemorial, He knows all, sees all, and has 'experienced' all. Remember, He was there before creation, He is, and He is to come— He knows the past, present and future, and importantly He lives in you. Let's consider some examples from the Bible. One of the reasons why Jesus was despised by the scribes and pharisees was because in their eyes, He lacked both the experience and the qualification— Jesus was all together Man, and all together God. Another example is David; although he also lacked these similar qualities of experience and qualification, skilled warriors—men of experience were drawn to him [I Chronicles 12]—David pursued God's heart! My last example is Paul. Read his letter to the Church in Rome, the Book of Romans. In Chapter 1: 11, Paul longs to see the Church, so that he may impart to them some spiritual gift. In verse 12, Paul also wants to be mutually encouraged, and in his personal greetings in Romans 16, Paul identifies two individuals, Andronicus and Junia [read verse 7]. These two came to know Christ before Paul did, yet Paul could boldly state that he was going to impart to them some spiritual gift. If length of time or age alone quantified superiority in experience, then all the examples of the people that I have mentioned would not have impacted the world.

I am convinced that Paul knew how fickle Man is and how people would struggle to receive a younger inexperienced preacher of the Word. When he sent Timothy to the Church at Corinth, he also wrote a letter to the Church [I Corinthians 4: 17], Paul said, "For this reason I have sent to you Timothy, my son whom I love, who is faithful in the Lord. He will remind you of my way of life in Christ, which agrees with what I teach everywhere in every church." Paul was endorsing Timothy but also encouraging the Church to accept and receive Timothy well.

Our experience must also see beyond our situations and circumstances. Our experiences must be of seeing God in everything and passing onto the next generation! Let's consider Asaph's contemplations in Psalm 78 [The Message]:

> Listen, dear friends, to God's truth,
> bend your ears to what I tell you.
> I'm chewing on the morsel of a proverb;
>   I'll let you in on the sweet old truths,
> Stories we heard from our fathers,
>   counsel we learned at our mother's knee.
> We're not keeping this to ourselves,
>   we're passing it along to the next generation—
> GOD's fame and fortune,
>   the marvellous things he has done.

He planted a witness in Jacob,
  set his Word firmly in Israel,
Then commanded our parents
  to teach it to their children
So the next generation would know,
  and all the generations to come—
Know the truth and tell the stories
  so their children can trust in God.
Never forget the works of God,
  but keep his commands to the letter.
Heaven forbid they should be like their parents,
  bull-headed and bad,
A fickle and faithless bunch
  who never stayed true to God.

The Ephraimites, armed to the teeth,
  ran off when the battle began.
They were cowards to God's Covenant,
  refused to walk by his Word.
They forgot what he had done—
  marvels he'd done right before their eyes.
He performed miracles in plain sight of their parents
  in Egypt, out on the fields of Zoan.
He split the Sea and they walked right through it;
  he piled the waters to the right and the left.
He led them by day with a cloud,
  led them all the night long with a fiery torch.
He split rocks in the wilderness,
  gave them all they could drink from underground springs;
He made creeks flow out from sheer rock,
  and water pour out like a river.

All they did was sin even more,
  rebel in the desert against the High God.
They tried to get their own way with God,

clamoured for favours, for special attention.
They whined like spoiled children,
Why can't God give us a decent meal in this desert?
Sure, he struck the rock and the water flowed,
  creeks cascaded from the rock.
But how about some fresh-baked bread?
  How about a nice cut of meat?"

When GOD heard that, he was furious—
  his anger flared against Jacob;
  he lost his temper with Israel.
It was clear they didn't believe God,
  had no intention of trusting in his help.
But God helped them anyway, commanded the clouds,
  and gave orders that opened the gates of heaven.
He rained down showers of manna to eat;
  he gave them the Bread of Heaven.
They ate the bread of the mighty angels;
  he sent them all the food they could eat.
He let East Wind break loose from the skies,
  gave a strong push to South Wind.
This time it was birds that rained down—
  succulent birds, an abundance of birds.
He aimed them right for the centre of their camp;
  all round their tents there were birds.
They ate and had their fill;
  he handed them everything they craved on a platter.
But their greed knew no bounds;
  they stuffed their mouths with more and more.
Finally, God was fed up, his anger erupted—
  he cut down their brightest and best,
  he laid low Israel's finest young men.

And—can you believe it?—they kept right on sinning;
  all those wonders and they still wouldn't believe!

So their lives wasted away to nothing—
  nothing to show for their lives but a ghost town.
When he cut them down, they came running for help;
  they turned and pled for mercy.
They gave witness that God was their rock,
  that High God was their redeemer,
But they didn't mean a word of it;
  they lied through their teeth the whole time.
They could not have cared less about him,
  wanted nothing to do with his Covenant.

And God? Compassionate!
  Forgave the sin! Didn't destroy!
Over and over he reined in his anger,
  restrained his considerable wrath.
He knew what they were made of;
  he knew there wasn't much to them.
How often in the desert they had spurned him,
  tried his patience in those wilderness years.
Time and again they pushed him to the limit,
  provoked Israel's Holy God.
How quickly they forgot what he'd done,
  forgot their day of rescue from the enemy,
When he did miracles in Egypt,
  wonders on the plain of Zoan.
He turned the River and its streams to blood—
  not a drop of water fit to drink.
He sent flies, which ate them alive,
  and frogs, which drove them crazy.
He turned their harvest over to caterpillars,
  everything they had worked for to the locusts.
He flattened their grapevines with hail;
  a killing frost ruined their orchards.
He pounded their cattle with hail,
  let thunderbolts loose on their herds.

His anger flared,
a wild firestorm of havoc,
An advance guard of disease-carrying angels
to clear the ground, preparing the way before him.
He didn't spare those people;
he let the plague rage through their lives.
He killed all the Egyptian firstborns,
lusty infants, offspring of Ham's virility.
Then he led his people out like sheep,
took his flock safely through the wilderness.
He took good care of them; they had nothing to fear.
The Sea took care of their enemies for good.
He brought them into his holy land;
this mountain he claimed for his own.
He scattered everyone who got in their way;
he staked out an inheritance for them—
the tribes of Israel all had their own places.

But they kept on giving him a hard time,
rebelled against God, the High God,
refused to do anything he told them.
They were worse, if that's possible, than their parents:
traitors—crooked as a corkscrew.
Their pagan orgies provoked God's anger;
their obscene idolatries broke his heart.
When God heard their carryings-on, he was furious;
he posted a huge No over Israel.
He walked off and left Shiloh empty,
abandoned the shrine where he had met with Israel.
He let his pride and joy go to the dogs,
turned his back on the pride of his life.
He turned them loose on fields of battle;
angry, he let them fend for themselves.
Their young men went to war and never came back;
their young women waited in vain.

Their priests were massacred,
  and their widows never shed a tear.

Suddenly, the Lord was up on his feet
  like someone roused from deep sleep,
  shouting like a drunken warrior.
He hit his enemies hard, sent them running,
  yelping, not daring to look back.
He disqualified Joseph as leader,
  told Ephraim he didn't have what it takes,
And chose the Tribe of Judah instead,
  Mount Zion, which he loves so much.
He built his sanctuary there, resplendent,
  solid and lasting as the earth itself.
Then he chose David, his servant,
  handpicked him from his work in the sheep pens.
One day, he was caring for the ewes and their lambs
  the next day God had him shepherding Jacob,
  his people Israel, his prize possession.
His good heart made him a good shepherd;
  he guided the people wisely and well.

Experience is to qualify by knowledge or practical wisdom gained from personally observing, encountering, or undergoing things as they occur in the course of time. It allows us to recognise, perceive, understand, and remember what we went through - whether we were successful or made errors and mistakes. As a result, we are a sum total of our experiences. Sometimes, things that we have undergone can shape and mould our ways of being and doing. For example, in the Bible, Joseph was a dreamer of dreams, and as he matured, he moved from self-centeredness and began to have a care and concern for others - he interpreted other people's dreams. His gift made room for him, and he subsequently interpreted Pharaoh's dream. Another example is Moses; he learned to shepherd Laban's sheep before shepherding Israel out of Egypt. Then there is David he fought the lion and bear, before he slew Goliath, preserved Israel's dignity, and then went on to be the Warrior King.

There is one thing that I know none of us are immune to, it's the fluctuations of life. I am yet to meet someone with the formula - show me that person, and I will show you a liar! Believe me, it would be lovely if life was always sunshine and roses. It would be good if life was always mountaintop after mountaintop, without grey skies and rain or dark valleys or naturally impassable rivers. Imagine everything going our way and always turning out right - wow! Unfortunately, life deals with punches of pain, losses, and we make mistakes and errors. David personally knew low moments in life. He said, "'Yea, though I walk through the valley of the shadow of death, I will fear no evil: for thou art with me; thy rod and thy staff, they comfort me.'" [Psalms 23: 4]. Then there is Jesus, He agonised and prayed, "My Father! If this cup cannot be taken away until I drink it, your will be done." [Matthew 26: 42]. Furthermore, Paul wrote to the Church at Corinth and said, "'We are pressed on every side by troubles, but we are not crushed and broken. We are perplexed, but we do not give up and quit.'" [II Corinthians 4: 8].

On the upside, we also have successes, victories, happiness, joy and laughter. All these are experiences. As a result, we must continually live life looking upwards and forwards, and every now and again, look backwards assessing life's lessons. Anyone who ever walks away from God or those living outside of Him, live predictable, cyclical, and visibly short-term lives. The reason for this is because when you live outside of God, you give the Devil foothold and control. He holds the deceived by the jugular vein, and ultimately, they are dangling puppets in his hand. Satan only has a limited number of tricks up his sleeve. His influence leads human events to always resemble those of preceding times. All you need to do is study the kings of Israel and Judah whose patterns were similar to Saul, the first man to be appointed king over God's people. Saul began as God's anointed [I Samuel 10] and ended up in witchcraft [I Samuel 28]. His departure from this life was miserable, as he committed suicide [I Samuel 31: 4].

If you are interested in a bit of modern Christian history, study the history of two great men of God—John Alexander Dowie who lived in the 1800s and William Marion Branham who lived in the 1900s. They lived in different eras, began well, but consider how they finished. God called them as prophets, He mightily used them, and both carried a strong anointing of the Holy Spirit. The latter's life repeated the exact same errors of his predecessor. God is gracious, and in their era, just as Samuel in the Bible warned and tried to steer Saul, God too sent other men and women to warn and steer these two men. When warnings go unheeded, when we ignore God's mercy, when we frivolously hold His grace, and choose to walk in wilful disobedience, such are the signs of defective or recessive genes in the House. You will invite death to your doorstep (Jude 5).

In Old Testament Israel, here is how they handled people who did not obey God. [Deuteronomy 21: 18 - 21] "If a man has a stubborn and rebellious son who will not obey the voice of his father or the voice of his mother, and, though they discipline him, will not listen to them, then his father and his mother shall take hold of him and bring him out to the elders of his city at the gate of the place where he lives, and they shall say to the elders of his city, 'This our son is stubborn and rebellious; he will not obey our voice; he is a glutton and a drunkard.' Then all the men of the city shall stone him to death with stones. So, you shall purge the evil from your midst, and all Israel shall hear, and fear." In the New Testament [our era], Ananias and Sapphira display the gravity of this [Acts 5: 1 - 11]. God will hand you over to Satan for the destruction of the flesh, so that your spirit is saved on judgement day [I Corinthians 5: 5]. God is serious; anyone who is going to mess with his Church, He will chastise. I hear the words echoing, just as Moses said to Pharaoh, concerning Israel [Exodus 4: 18 - 23], "The Church is my Bride. Do not contaminate her, or else, I will kill you!" We must endeavour to do what God requires of us and not lead God's people into error. A generation is endorsed as responsible when it passes on its gained experience [knowledge and revelation acted upon], to the subsequent generation. Those who follow need to analyse, learn, and understand yesteryear's experiences. When there is a group of men and women of God together, there is a wealth of experience. There is an aggregation of God moments, a higher concentration of faith, greater expectations, and a tangible presence of God that infuses and shifts the atmosphere. If this mix is met with an unquenchable desire to share, transfer, impact, and pass on to the coming generations, it will make it easier and faster for subsequent generations to begin the journey of maturity.

In Psalm 127: 4 - 5, the warrior or archer represents all initiators who choose to hit the target. Arrows represent sons, daughters, mentees, the inexperienced and youth who must never be wasted. Every shot must strike a blow to the adversary and lead to victory. I heard that to be a skilled archer it takes years of practice, to hit the target successfully and consistently. You must observe the wind speed, wind direction, gauge the distance, and learn when and how to take the shot. It is called experience. The releasing of the arrow is like catapulting sons into the future. Have you ever observed an arrow in flight? Arrows are designed for aerodynamics. They are made to travel in the air with the least amount of resistance possible. They are light enough to carry and do not have dead weight, and most importantly, arrows have sharp tips, so that when they hit their target, they penetrate with a killer blow. Sons who are sharpened, travel with brute force and without inhibition hit the mark. In II Kings 3:11-12, when King Jehoshaphat heard about Elisha, who had served Elijah, his response was definitive for he knew that the Elijah spiritual "DNA" had been transmitted.

To qualify means to have the necessary skills, knowledge, and credentials. Acquiring a literacy or educational qualification does not mean competency, and neither does it guarantee a successful future in the attained qualification. Competency is demonstrated by applying oneself in the role or function.

I would like to describe two incidents that changed my life forever. In 1996, in my final year of studying Mineral Processing & Extractive Metallurgy, we went on a field trip and visited, at that time one of the largest gold-producing mines in Zimbabwe. There was a gentleman plant metallurgist who took our group around the metallurgical plant. His knowledge was superior, and he impressed us all. After a couple of hours of touring the plant, as we sat around a table for lunch, one of my colleagues asked the metallurgist about his educational credentials and qualifications. The gentleman explained that he was "QBE"— qualified by experience. It was, however, my colleagues' subsequent negative reaction toward his response, which made me appreciate the importance of using your gift, pursuing your passion and then, growing your experience. A lack of educational qualification did not make this man any less in his ability. This gentleman was brilliant and yet held no formal qualification. He was a good teacher too, and the excellent production figures of the metallurgical plant reflected this. In contrast, months later, having qualified and graduated and now working as a metallurgist, I collaborated with an experienced plant foreman. He had been working in this metallurgical plant for over thirty years; he had a wealth of experience and was very efficient. However, this man was not a team player. He was selfish. He refused to teach or share information and had a disregard and lack of respect for any graduate. As I reflected on these two men, I concluded that an individual's passion and intelligence [or general mental ability] are some key factors to determine one's productivity in a role or function. Both men had clearly used their God-given gifts differently. What clearly set them apart was character. One had character, and the other did not. However, what struck me most was that, in the two different companies, someone identified each of them, saw their respective potentials, looked beyond their lack of formal qualification, and recruited them. Experience and qualification must always be held in tension.

My experience reminded me of Solomon's son Rehoboam. When Rehoboam had become King, he ignored the wise counsel of the old men who had advised Solomon [I Kings 12: 6 - 8]. Instead, he followed the counsel of young men. Rehoboam subsequently became a ruthless taskmaster; his actions came to nought, and as a result his kingdom was divided.

You have probably heard it said that if you do something well [whatever it is], and really lead others well, the measurement of how well you do is seen in those you have led, especially when you are absent or gone. They are supposed to either maintain the same level or better the level of performance. If standards deteriorate, it is one of three things; firstly, you either keep everything to yourself and are self-centred. Secondly, you failed to identify, recruit, and train well. Thirdly, those you manage or trained are ignorant and are time wasters. In this regard, let me give you two fascinating modern day illustrations of continuity of experience and their subsequent impact.

Have you heard about Brooklyn Bridge, which connects Brooklyn and Manhattan in the United States of America? The videos and photos I have seen of it are amazing. There is, however, a story from conception to construction. The bridge's architect was John Roebling, who sadly died before the construction began. John's son Washington Roebling, who had worked with him on several other bridges and helped design the Brooklyn Bridge, took over the responsibility as chief engineer to oversee the construction. In 1883, fourteen years after commencement of construction, the bridge was completed, and it still stands today. Although John died and never saw the physical manifestation, he still receives the credit. Can you imagine if John's vision was temporary and only centred around himself? What would have happened if he had been selfish and not identified his son or anyone else? Would the bridge have ever been constructed? John triggered a ripple which has become wave after wave. Generations have reaped and continue to reap the benefits from use of the bridge.

My second example is Sir Christopher Wren, one of the founding members of the well-known Royal Society, a Fellowship of many of the world's most eminent scientists and is the oldest scientific academy in continuous existence. He was a designer, astronomer, physicist, geometrician, and the most highly acclaimed English architect. After the Great Fire of London in 1666, Sir Christopher Wren was instrumental in reconstructing numerous buildings and is acknowledged as being responsible for the rebuilding of about 52 church buildings. Sir Christopher Wren is however famously known for the design and commencement of construction of St Paul's Cathedral, London in 1675. 35 years later, in 1710, St Paul's Cathedral was completed and still stands today. He handed the baton to others, to finish the construction, and died in 1723. Generations witnessed the construction, and to date, generations enjoy use of the facility. Continuity was initiated by his father, also called Christopher Wren, a priest in the Church who died in 1659. Christopher senior trained his son [Proverbs 22: 6] to be an architect. Christopher senior must have identified God's gift and call on his son. Senior provided the wood and oil, and young Christopher stirred up the gift [II Timothy 1: 6]. Although Christopher junior was a brilliant mind in other technical fields, it is the area of his father's identification and nurture that he is well known for.

In I Corinthians 1: 1, Paul introduces himself as "CALLED to be an apostle of Christ Jesus, by the will of God." Although Paul had been well schooled under Gamaliel, a man who was held in high regard as a Jewish teacher of the Law [Acts 22: 3], notice how when Paul wrote his letter to the Church in Philippians 3: 8, amongst other things, he considers all the things he did or accomplished in the flesh, prior to knowing Christ [including his "education"], to be rubbish! It is the CALLING of God that became his turning point, as well as his drive. Romans 11: 29 says that the gifts and CALLING of God are irrevocable. Paul had gained head knowledge in the flesh, perhaps equivalent to our modern-day qualifications, but still murdered people, in ignorance. In verse 2 of I Corinthians 1, Paul then transfers the attention of calling from himself to the Church, Paul says, "to those sanctified in Christ and CALLED to be his holy people..." That is, you and me! Our only qualification is being IN CHRIST [1 John 4: 4]. If you go through the New Testament and count the number of times IN CHRIST or IN HIM is stated or inferred, it is over 130 times. Now let's compare, Paul who in the flesh was well schooled, and put him against Peter, who in the flesh was an [uneducated] fisherman [Matthew 4]. Together with John, Peter is also described as an ordinary man [Acts 4: 13]. Jesus is the differentiator! Jesus is also the equaliser! When you are in Him, and follow His call, you will walk in the perfect will of God. What you have or don't have outwardly becomes non-existent. We will celebrate our callings, differences, as well as spur each other on. Now notice too, that Peter also states this in his letter, I Peter 1: 1 "Peter an apostle of Jesus of Christ...." What has God called you to be? A Pastor? A Doctor? An Administrator? A Sportsperson? Do it for the glory God [Colossians 3: 23] and impact your sphere, for Jesus Christ. Look beyond your external qualifications. Qualifications can sometimes give a perception which is not the reality. Especially in the 21st century, people love titles, and the gullible are quickly deceived.

Qualifications do not guarantee 100% performance. Let me give you a personal example. I once worked for a top global bank as a private banker and became one of the top performers. It is possible to outsmart and outperform colleagues who have a chain of banking qualifications. Qualifications alone should never be used as a measure of an individual's ability or output. In addition, experience alone does not result in an individual outperforming those without. Gifts and calling must be honed through learning, and where possible by attending school, college, university, or submissively learning from those that have the applied knowledge or experience - this will add value. I am sure you will agree with me that if you want to be a practicing medical doctor, and that is your calling, you must aim to get to university. We must understand our individual callings, know our gifts, sharpen those gifts, learn from the experienced, and in turn acquire the experience for ourselves.

The most important thing is obedience to the call of God. Don't run another man's race. Stick to your lane. When in the race, focus on the prize ahead. Never compete or measure yourself against another. Callings of God are different, graces as well as degrees of anointing are also different. Furthermore, manifestations are as the Holy Spirit wills, so never manufacture anything. Let Jesus be your fulcrum, yield completely to the leading of the Holy Spirit, and know the love of the Father, so that you in turn walk in the love of God. Remember, faith without works is dead, and knowledge that is not acted upon is just information.

Recorded in the Bible too, we see how Jesus was on occasion confronted about His credentials:

John 10: 24 - 26 (AMP)
So, the Jews surrounded Him and began asking Him, "How long are You going to keep us in doubt and suspense? If You are really the Christ (the Messiah), tell us so plainly and openly. Jesus answered them, "I have told you so, yet you do not believe Me [you do not trust Me and rely on Me]. The very works that I do by the power of My Father and in My Father's name bear witness concerning Me [they are My credentials and evidence in support of Me]. But you do not believe and trust and rely on Me because you do not belong to My fold [you are no sheep of Mine]."

Jesus was clearly being regarded as young and inexperienced because he was in his early thirties [Luke 3: 23]. In those days the norm was that a Jewish rabbi would have been someone much older, who was considered to have more information, qualifications, and numerous years of experience. As a result, the Jews wanted Jesus to produce His credentials and evidence that He was the Messiah. After being saved, Paul himself refused to buckle to the external pressure of having to prove his "credentials"; he only presented himself to Peter and James.

It is recorded in Galatians 1: 18 - 22: "Then three years later, I did go up to Jerusalem to become personally acquainted with Peter, and remained with him for fifteen days, but I did not see any of the other apostles except James, the brother of our Lord. Now, I write this as if I were standing before the bar of God; I do not lie. Then I went into the districts of Syria and Cilicia and so far, I was still unknown by sight to the churches of Christ in Judea."

The Church must never play catch-up to the world. We are supposed to be at the forefront, the forerunners. Several years ago, very dear friends of ours who live in London, England visited us, and during a conversation, they informed my wife and I that their then five-year-old son had been scouted by a London-based Premier League football club – a well-known football club. Tell me that is not impressive? The world is continuously identifying and planning succession. Surely, the Church needs even higher standards than these? Continuity is identifying, taking through induction, providing an environment for growing competency, encouraging higher levels of excellence, and then strategically setting out succession plans. Let me just add something here, to demonstrate how the Church sometimes plays catch-up, or even gets trounced by the world: There was a prominent man of God who for years impacted the world with his teaching. In one day, this man, and senior members of his team died. You are probably thinking or asking the question: 'What became of the work began in him?' My response to you is simple - your guess is as good as mine. The reality is that each of us has been handpicked by God. Even before conception, God knew each of us. None of us is a surprise or accident to God. We are here to impact someone, to the glory of God.

The day we entered earth, we were born with God's dreams, vision, and purpose. Sadly, most people never discover these. Our first step must always be to ask God.

Now learn to number your days, that you may gain a heart of wisdom [Psalm 90: 12]. You need to maximise your time and fully utilise your God-given gift [Matthew 25: 14 - 30]. The Bible says that God has freely given gifts, which we did not earn or work hard for, will make room for us and bring us before kings [Proverbs 18: 16]. This scripture is both figurative and literal; Bezalel and Oholiab who were great craftsmen were brought to Moses [Exodus 31], Joseph an interpreter of dreams interpreted pharaoh's dream [Genesis 41], David a skilled musician was brought before King Saul [I Samuel 16: 14 - 23], Daniel, who was endowed with wisdom and understanding visions, stood before the King of Babylon [Daniel 2], and Paul an intellect and learned scholar knew his rights as Roman citizen appealed unto Caesar [Acts 25: 11] and preached Christ in Rome, unreservedly. Conversely, in the world, currency is used as a measure of value as well as a medium of exchange and, unfortunately, the same thinking has been placed on educational qualifications. Skills are now being considered as the true measure of ability; for example, when you apply for a job, they state minimum requirements such as five GCSEs including Mathematics and English. Not everyone will obtain the so-called minimum requirements, and that does not make one a failure. Some of the world's biggest brands and companies were kick-started by individuals who do not meet the so-called minimum requirements. This begs the question: Who initiated this type of thinking?

Never underestimate the gift of God. Through exposure, we gain experience and then go on to excel. The truth is that we need to blend gift, skill, and experiences with qualification to do the significant things of God. Let us not overrate qualification [I also know people who have qualifications and yet have no ability in the subject. Some were coerced, and others studied just to please someone]. Lest I am misinterpreted and misunderstood, let me be clear. I am not against qualifications. I am a graduate and worked very hard—my message is that one size does not fit all. The irony is that the Bible says, 'The race is not to the swift or the battle to the strong, nor does food come to the wise or wealth to the brilliant or favour to the learned; but time and chance happen to us all' [Ecclesiastes 9: 11]. This verse is also not an excuse for people to hide behind 'time and chance,' also remember that the Bible says, 'A labourer is worthy of his hire'. Someone should be properly paid for their work or effort [Luke 10: 7].

Clearly, God's ways are higher than our ways [Isaiah 55: 8 - 9]. Man qualifies by outward appearance, yet God looks at the heart [I Samuel 16: 7]. If qualification in the kingdom was done in the same manner as the world, would the twelve disciples have qualified? For example, Peter, Andrew, James, and John were fishermen; Matthew was a tax collector, and Simon was a zealot [a rebel]. Compare and contrast by qualification a couple of individuals in the Bible. Samuel [I Samuel 1: 11], a boy prophet, was raised in the House of God. Look at Josiah [2 Kings 22]—an eight-year-old King of Judah. Consider Paul [Acts 22: 3]—a pharisee who studied under Gamaliel and was thoroughly trained in the Law, as well as being a tentmaker [Acts 18:3]. Look at Jesus Christ [Matthew 13: 55]—a carpenter, the Anointed One.

We should sharpen our gifts and become skilful through practice, training, studying and acquiring knowledge. The Bible encourages us to hone our God-given gifts: study to show yourself approved [II Timothy 2: 15]; meditate on the Word [Joshua 1: 8] and play skilfully [Psalm 33: 3]. Even a talented footballer spends hours perfecting the penalty kick or free kick—they call it muscle memory. A musician will hone their singing ability or instrument playing through hours of constant practice, and the person who intends to get the qualification will immerse themselves in their studies for hours while others sleep, play or procrastinate. It is character, however, that will take a person even further.

Did you know that in most major financial institutions around the world or major economies, they document events, strategies, and methods applied in the past to produce a winning formula eventually? Their record-keeping and archiving are systematic and impeccable. They are always searching for areas to improve. If you are young or new in a role and seeking to implement change, you have a wealth of documented evidence [experience] as a measure. This strategy ensures that there is no repetition of past errors and mistakes [due to wilful disobedience, ignorance, or selfishness]. Let us take a lesson from when the custodian was with Esther [Esther 2: 12]; let us apply many oils and perfumes to the coming generations [anointing and mantle passing on]—oil of walking with and in God, oil of faith, oil of healing, oil of joy and oil of prosperity. Let us show them our crowns of victories, as well as scars from our errors and mistakes, so that in their future interactions, they will walk in a new measure of authority and in unimaginable realms with God. The Church is to mature, impact, change, transform, and demonstrate Christ here on earth until Jesus returns for His Bride.

II Chronicles 20: 13-15 (AMP)
*And all Judah stood before the Lord, with their children and their wives. Then the Spirit of the Lord came upon **Jahaziel, son of Zechariah**, the son of Benaiah, the son of Jeiel, the son of Mattaniah, a Levite of the sons of Asaph, in the midst of the assembly. He [Jahaziel] said, "Hearken, all Judah, you inhabitants of Jerusalem, and you King Jehoshaphat. The Lord says this to you: 'Be not afraid or dismayed at this great multitude; for the battle is not yours, but God's.'"*

In the past when I had heard the story, all credit has been to King Jehoshaphat, for his obedience. In this book, I also want to pay tribute to others not often recognised and acknowledged. These men poured their experiences and imparted, so that each generation continued to walk with God. It is like a pouring of the Spirit and all experiences, so that the next generation does things faster, quicker, and better. You see, in these verses, it all began with Asaph. I have read numerous thoughts written by Asaph in the Book of Psalms, including his contemplation Psalm 78. His passion for God and continuity flows through the generations all the way to the prophet Zechariah. On that day, when it seemed the nation of Judah would be overrun, Jahaziel, the son of the prophet Zechariah, spoke by the Spirit of God, and God wrought victory. Had Asaph not set the ball of continuity in motion, Judah would have been frightened to death. Picture a pouring transferring, an impartation, and the gathering of momentum from:

Asaph [which means "the gatherer"] to **Mattaniah** [which means "God's gift"] to **Benaiah** [which means "God builds up"] to **Zechariah** [which means "the one whom God remembers"] and finally, **Jahaziel** [which means "the one who is beheld by God"]. The baton was transferred and embraced in this lineage.

I want to appreciate Zechariah, the son of Benaiah, for not buckling to the world around him. He was God-focused and refused to bow or bend to any new patterns. Instead, he held the course maintained his family lineage and impacted his son, Jahaziel, encouraging him to go further. It is not a coincidence that God names Zechariah's family in this chapter. I believe that all who are named in verse 14 had something so different in their "DNA" that God saw it fit to mention each by name. They had continuity etched in their hearts and minds. Zechariah, through his son Jahaziel, was responsible for a pivotal event in the history of the nation of Judah.

In contrast to the above, once upon a time, Babylon was ruling the known world and had also captured and led the children of God into captivity. Israel was no more, just a desolate place with its place in history. Upon arresting the sons of God, the Babylonian ruling party, and then the government under the rulership of Nebuchadnezzar handpicked some select Jews for government service. Amongst those selected was Daniel. I want to focus on Nebuchadnezzar and his family.

In Nebuchadnezzar was a powerful king ruler, not just a country but an empire. Babylon had conquered and was now running over and controlling most of the known world. His ruling was one of compromising and mixing a broad range of practices, rituals, self-belief, and self-exaltation. He combined being secular; he wanted to be a god and believed in and accommodated magic, followed sorcery, tolerated the occult, converting selected men into eunuchs, had time for astrology for guidance and also threw into the mix, adhering to the instructions of the God of Daniel. Nebuchadnezzar experienced much during his reign: from strange, heart-wrenching, disturbing dreams to instructing three young Hebrew men to be thrown into a fiery furnace; from arrogance, self-exaltation and seeing himself as a god, to leaving the royal palace and living like a beast, feeding on grass. Can you picture the talk in the empire? "The king has gone mad..." Then came the restoration of the man: Nebuchadnezzar's restoration, acknowledgement, and proclamation that there is one true God, the God of Daniel.

Between chapter 4 and chapter 5 of the Book of Daniel, there was a transition of power between father and son, from Nebuchadnezzar to Belshazzar. The obvious is that Belshazzar must have been earmarked to rule at some stage. What is hazy and not clear is his ability to learn from his father's mistakes and experiences and to do things better. Instead, we see almost a cycle: We pick up a sense of pride, arrogance, and a love for magicians, astrologers, Chaldeans, and soothsayers. The question is: Was he not present when his father experienced the dreams, the pride, the fiery furnace and the insanity, the restoration and most importantly, Nebuchadnezzar's acknowledgement of the God of the Hebrews? Did his father [Nebuchadnezzar] not teach or instruct him?

Daniel 5: 1 - 6 (NLT)

Many years later, King Belshazzar hosted a great feast for 1,000 of his nobles, and he drank wine with them. While Belshazzar was drinking the wine, he gave orders to bring in the gold and silver cups that his predecessor, Nebuchadnezzar, had taken from the Temple in Jerusalem. He wanted to drink from them with his nobles, his wives, and his concubines. So, they brought these gold cups, taken from the Temple, the house of God in Jerusalem, and the king and his nobles, his wives, and his concubines drank from them. While they drank from them, they praised their idols made of gold, silver, bronze, iron, wood, and stone. Suddenly, they saw the fingers of a human hand, writing on the plaster wall of the king's palace, near the lampstand. The king himself saw the hand as it wrote, and his face turned pale with fright. His knees knocked together in fear, and his legs gave way beneath him.

Belshazzar had committed a worse offence than his father. In his pride and arrogance, to elevate and showcase his might and power and to belittle his guests, I can just picture him, instructing the servants to collect the golden cups taken from the Temple, the house of the Hebrews' God, in Jerusalem. What he did not realise was that this great God had become the God of his father, Nebuchadnezzar [Daniel Chapter 5: 17 - 23]. I think Belshazzar was trying to establish a new world order and wanted to be likened to a god. He probably thought that the Hebrews' God was no more. That very night, Belshazzar was weighed and found wanting and God stripped away the kingdom of Babylon. The family heritage of leaders was immediately cut off. Was God ruthless? Not at all: it is a lesson for us to share our life experiences - errors and mistakes, victories, and successes - and not to be ashamed to tell others about where we disobeyed God.

In comparison, King Xerxes a Persian [who also dominated the known world at a different point in history], also from a dynasty presented himself better than Belshazzar the Babylonian. The Bible says that one night the king could not sleep, and he gave orders to bring the Book of Memorable Deeds, the Chronicles, to be read before him, and it was found written how Mordecai had told about Bigthana and Teresh, two of the king's eunuchs, who guarded the threshold, and who had sought to lay hands on King Xerxes [Esther 6:1-2 ESV]. It made him better understand some of the history of his nation as well as realise the false accusation against the inhabitants of Judah and Jerusalem. One of the heroes of his empire, Mordecai, was still alive, and he had never been acknowledged or formally decorated. Upon this revelation, king Xerxes ultimately honoured God's people. One man [Xerxes] prolonged his reign and the rule of his empire Persia, and another man [Mordecai] saved the Hebrews from complete annihilation. Both men were pioneers and initiators who impacted generations. Remember, you have the same ability residing in you.

Thabani Nyoni

COVENANT RELATIONSHIPS

Genesis 50:19 - 21

But Joseph told them [his brothers], "Don't be afraid of me. Am I God, to judge and punish you? As far as I am concerned, God turned into good what you meant for evil. He brought me to the high position I have today, so I could save the lives of many people. Now therefore fear not; I will nourish you, and your children. And he comforted them [his brothers] and spoke kindly unto them.

John 19:26 - 27 *(ESV)*

When Jesus saw his mother and the disciple whom he loved standing nearby, he said to his mother, "Woman, behold, your son!" Then he said to the disciple, "Behold, your mother!" And from that hour the disciple took her to his own home.

In Genesis, we learn that Joseph not only saved his brothers, but their households and subsequent generations. He made a pledge and honoured or fulfilled his words. That which Joseph did was indeed quite prophetic. His acts were but a shadow of the works of Christ. Through Jesus Christ, we and all our children and those that are to come to Him and receive Him as Lord and Saviour are saved and will be nourished. His covenant with us is forever. As you look at the verse from the Book of John, out of the twelve disciples He handpicked, Jesus chose John to be the one who would look after His mother, Mary, when He was gone. Was there anything wrong with the others? Definitely not! His relationship with each of them was different, and He still loved them all. In His worst hour - of beatings leading to crucifixion, where was Peter, James, or the other disciples? Yet in the distance stood John, with Mary. Jesus established a covenant relationship, which both Mary and John responded to. The very hour Jesus gave the instruction, John took Mary as his mother and brought her into his home.

70

My question to you is one that has already been asked by God: Can two people walk together without agreeing on the direction [Amos 3: 3]? God established relationships before the foundation of the earth. The first level relationship is that of the Godhead - Father, Son, and Holy Spirit [three distinct persons, yet one]. The day Adam was created by God, another level of the relationship came into being between the Godhead and Man. Furthermore, when God realised that Adam was alone, he took something out of the Man and created the woman [Eve]; thus, another relationship was birthed between a man and woman. As a result of the union between a man and woman, their offspring came forth, brothers Cain and Abel. From this, two more relationships came into existence: the parent-child relationship as well as the sibling relationship. The other relationship we see in the Bible is between David and Jonathan—a true friendship. In all these various levels of relationships, we recognise that God is at the centre of each; He is a God of *covenant*.

There are several covenants found in the Bible, including:

- The covenant with Adam and Eve in the Garden of Eden [Genesis 2: 15 - 17]
- The covenant with Noah – after the flood destruction [Genesis 9: 8 - 17]
- The covenant with Abraham [Genesis 15: 8, 17:9]
- The covenant with Isaac [Genesis 17: 19, 21]
- The covenant with Jacob [Genesis 28: 16]
- The covenant with Israel after deliverance from Egypt [Exodus 20 – 24]
- The covenant with David – his descendants to be Israel's throne [II Sam 7: 11- 16]
- The New Covenant [Jeremiah 31: 31–33; Matthew 26:28; Mark 14: 24; Luke 22: 20; I Corinthians 11: 25; II Corinthians 3: 6; Hebrews 9: 15]

Man's first covenant relationship must always be with God. Our covenant with God is the foundational relationship, above all other relationships. He is a covenant keeping God who desires a relationship. In the Old Testament, when two parties made a pact, the two would kill an animal, divide it in two, and then stand on either side of the isolated animal facing each other. They would then make declarations to each other, each person declaring all that they had and owned, and agree that from that moment, they were one man—co-owners who shared what each had previously owned. After this, they walked around the sacrifice in a figure of eight. The number eight in the Bible symbolises new beginnings and a bright future. They would usually slit their hands and shake with the same bleeding hand. From that moment, the two became one, symbolically. They would also declare to each other that if they became covenant breakers, God should do to each of them as they had done to the animal.

The New Covenant is based on better promises of redemption by God to people as individuals rather than as a nation. Rather than a person's adherence to the law, it is by God's grace, through Jesus Christ, who is the Mediator of the new covenant, [read Hebrews 8: 6-13]. Symbolically, when Jesus was crucified, He was the sacrificial lamb; the two robbers on either side of Him represent us. Jesus' outstretched arms and pierced hands reached out to the two robbers. Similarly, His outstretched hands reach out to each of us. Jesus Christ is the Mediator and the Author of the New Covenant. The psalmist reminds us that:

*Know therefore that the Lord your God is God; He is the faithful God, keeping His covenant of love **to a thousand generations** of those who love Him and keep His commandments.* [Deuteronomy 7: 9]

The word covenant is one of the most frequently used words in the Bible. A covenant is a promise, a pact, a treaty, or a written *agreement*, usually solemn and formal, between two or more people to do or not do something specified. This agreement is a binding necessity. An agreement is a situation in which people share the same opinion; it is also a contract by which people agree about what is to be done. Agreement also speaks of accord, unity, or harmony. I like the word *harmony*; it describes a pleasing combination or arrangement of different musical notes played or sung at the same time to produce a symphony or unified pleasant sound. As individuals who are walking in covenant, we each are unique musical transcripts. We need to hit our notes so that we blend in with others and create a lasting symphony. Harmony means that we may have different styles and administration, but when we walk in agreement, we share the same vision and values. Where unity and accord exist, God commands a blessing [Psalm 133: 1 - 3].

God will never override the will of Man. Although He has plans, thoughts, intentions, and a will for each of us, it is up to us to align ourselves with Him. When we allow God to order our steps, and we walk according to His purpose, all things work together for our good, whether in relationships or other areas of life. Pursue God until He tells you what to do next. I want to emphasise that a person is not worthy of being your spouse, friend, or business partner simply by being a Christian. We should never just jump into relationships. Let God decide everything in your life. Remember, the Bible reminds us that you were fearfully and wonderfully made—you are special [Psalm 139: 14]. We are to also keep away [not hate or despise], from brothers or sisters in the Church that walk disorderly [II Thessalonians 3: 6]. So, sadly, even brothers or sisters in the Lord can live disastrous or topsy-turvy lives. Let us be God conscious in all types of relationships, and always follow God's lead [Romans 8:14]. If we do not consult Him, sooner or later, we will end up in trouble.

Let me give you a personal illustration. Years ago, I pursued self-employment and partnered with Christian brothers. I had big dreams. At the time, it seemed good to me to proceed, but I did not consult God. I eventually walked away from the business not only with nothing, but I also carried a huge financial debt. I was out of work, without income for three and a half years. I literally cried out to God. Everywhere I searched, doors were shut, and no one gave me the office job and posts that I had previously held. God broke me like a skilled cowboy breaks a wild stallion. I threw aside personal reputation and dignity. I rolled up my sleeves, took a basin and towel, and learned all over again. I was ever so grateful as God opened a door for me. I worked in a grocery store, not serving friendly smiling customers. They gave me a role in the back, packing shelves, replenishing the aisles late at night when the shop was closed. I worked 11-hour nightshifts. If I detailed the treatment I received, we would have a pity party. Angry? No. Regret? No. God straightened me out, and ever since, I have learned and yielded into walking in obedience. God has opened doors, ever since. Now, the reason for my illustration is to encourage you, always walk in covenant with God, make sure you have heard from God every step.

Outside of covenant relationships, everything you do is temporary. Remember the prodigal son [Luke 15: 11 - 32]? Outside of his father he withered, cracked, fell to below pig standard, and lay wasted. He eventually came to his senses and went back to his father. His father gave him a ring for his finger —a covenant. The Father says, "You are His signet ring [Haggai 2: 23]; will you and your seed remain on His finger?"

God's desire is that we walk in covenant relationships. Covenant relationships are built on love, respect, accountability, openness, security, and often stand the test of time. There are people whom we will encounter, and it may be for just one season. They will impact our lives or vice versa. Then there are others with whom we have an extended divine connection; these are part of our journey or destiny. It is important that we discern, distinguish, and identify these people, and finally, proceed to forge covenant relationships. We need to teach coming generations, and most importantly, they need to see our lives as examples. The Bible says:

Isaiah 59:21
*"As for Me," says the Lord, "this is My **covenant** with them [YOU]: My Spirit who is upon you, and My words, which I have put in your mouth, shall not depart from your mouth, nor from the mouth of your*

descendants, nor from the mouth of your descendants' descendants,"
says the Lord, "from this time and forevermore."

God is so serious about His covenant that He says, "I will not violate
my covenant or alter the word that went forth from my lips." [Psalm
89: 34]. Just as He is, so must we be, let us therefore not be covenant
breakers, but instead, build for eternity.

COVENANT: FRIENDSHIPS

"A man who has friends **must show himself** to be friendly..."
[Proverbs 18: 24a] The second part of the same verse tells us that
some friends only bring loss, and yet, there is a friend more loyal
than a brother. When I look at the life of David, I am reminded that he
had older brothers who served in King Saul's army. David's brothers
had natural presence and stature—they must have had an aura about
them. None of them seemed to look out for their younger brother. Do
you remember the day of anointing by Samuel? None of them took
notice or even recognised that their youngest brother David had not
been summoned to the meeting. Can you picture that? Same father,
same mother, but no one realising your absence? It is likely that none
of the brothers took notice of, or understood the teenage David, until
he stood before Goliath and then entered the king's residence to
serve. Could there have been an element of envy or jealousy by the
brothers? Did they know of the exploits of David when tending the
sheep? Did they believe him when he told them about the lion and the
bear? [I Samuel 17: 34 - 37]. After all, they had all been present when
the prophet Samuel had visited the house of Jesse to anoint next king
of Israel [I Samuel 16: 13].

Unlike the relationship he had with his brothers—his own flesh and
blood—the covenant relationship made between David and Jonathan
[II Samuel 21:7] extended to another generation. Even when Jonathan
was dead, David treated Mephibosheth, Jonathan's son, as his own
son [II Samuel 9: 10].

Here are some nuggets that we learn about real friendships:

Samuel 18: 1, 3, & 4 (ESV)
1. As soon as he had finished speaking to Saul, the soul of Jonathan was knit to the soul of David, and Jonathan loved him as his soul.
3. Then Jonathan made a covenant with David because he loved him as his soul.
4 And Jonathan stripped himself of the robe that was on him and gave it to David, and his armour, his sword, and his bow, and his belt.

- Friends love unconditionally and are open and transparent [verse 1 & 3b].
- Friends share their belongings [verse 4].
- Friends are often open, honest, and expressive [verse 3a].
- Friends look out, protect, and bring out the best in each other [I Samuel 19: 2 - 7].
- Friendship extends through generations [II Samuel 9: 1 – 10 and II Samuel 21: 7].
- Friends sharpen and encourage each other to grow in faith [Proverbs 27: 17].

If we do not pass on the baton [of friendship], here is what may happen in the coming generations:

II Samuel 10: 1 - 4
And it came to pass after this that the king of the children of Ammon died, and Hanun his son reigned in his stead. Then said David, "I will show kindness unto Hanun the son of Nahash, as his father showed kindness unto me." And David sent to comfort him by the hand of his servants for his father. And David's servants came into the land of the children of Ammon. And the princes of the children of Ammon said unto Hanun their lord, "Thinkest thou that David doth honour thy father, that he hath sent comforters unto thee? Hath not David rather sent his servants unto thee to search the city and to spy it out and to overthrow it?" Therefore, Hanun took David's servants and shaved

off one half of their beards and cut off their garments in the middle, even to their buttocks, and sent them away.

It is difficult to comprehend how, in one generation, David and Nahash, king of the Ammonites forged an alliance and lived peaceably in one season, and barely before his father's corpse had even decomposed, Hanun violated the allegiance. Logically, you would have expected the relationship of the Israelites and the Ammonites to have blossomed and stood the test of time. Other generations arose who did not know the history of this key covenant friendship. By Hanun instructing that David's servants have their beards shaved, he was removing their dignity. Beards were part of their hallmark and identity. In fact, it was customary for Jewish men to anoint their heads and beard. Can you imagine what it meant to these men and David. Exposing their buttocks was a clear sign of disrespect and embarrassment. Holding lightly a friendship that had endured, resulted in the death of thousands of Ammonites [read the rest of Chapter 10].

COVENANT: MARRIAGE

Marriage is a God-instituted covenant. Marriage is the relationship that exists between a husband [Man] and wife [Woman] - In Mark 10: 7 - 9. A few years ago, this would have been an obvious statement—not so in these times. Contrary to so much of what we are beginning to hear in mainstream media and the worldly pressure to redefine marriage, there is no other version of marriage in the eyes of God. The Author of life says it, and it is so. His Message will never change. It is not about how I feel; it is everything to do with what God says. We do not hate, despise, or look down on other people's views or stances— We are a Bible believing people. The Church must never lose its voice—nor compromise, regardless of how high the temperature gets elevated—and it is going to get even hotter!

The Bible is clear, 'He who created them from the beginning made them Male and Female, and said, 'For this reason a man shall leave his father and mother and be joined to his wife [*a woman*], and the two shall become one flesh' So they are no longer two, but one flesh. What therefore God has joined together let no man separate' [Matthew 19: 4 - 6]. Marriage is the union of a Man and a Woman. Anything outside of this is a sin. Let's see what God says, 'You shall not lie with a male as one lies with a female; it is an abomination. Also, you shall not have intercourse with any animal to be defiled with it, nor shall any woman stand before an animal to mate with it; it is a perversion.' [Leviticus 18: 22 - 23]. The Bible reminds us that there is nothing new under the sun [Ecclesiastes 1: 9]. Just when you think you are doing something that is unique to this century—let me burst your bubble, you're not. Satan only has a limited number of tricks, and they are cyclical. In fact, when Paul wrote his letter to the Church in Rome, he touched on this matter, read Romans 1: 26 – 32. Let me further disappoint plenty of people, marriage is not cohabiting; people who are not married should remain single until the day they get married. Abstain from sex until marriage.

The Book of Genesis allows us to see beautifully painted pictures of marriage; with God presenting Eve to Adam [Genesis 2:22], and also Abraham making his servant swear that he would find a wife for his son Isaac amongst his kinsman, [read Genesis 24]. Abraham did not want his son to mix with a Canaanite. As a result, we see the coming together of Isaac and Rebekah. Furthermore, we see how passionate about marriage God is when He tells Husbands [a Man] to love their wives [a Woman] as Christ loves the Church, [Ephesians 5:21-33]. The Church is the Bride, and Jesus Christ is the Bridegroom. It must follow that the union between a bride and bridegroom is holy. Now observe how loose modern society handle marital relationships no wonder the world is in a mess. Marriage is not debatable; the Church is not supposed to be confused on the matter. We did not write The Holy Bible—God did. Christians are not imposing anything on the world, neither are we criticising or looking down on anyone. We are demonstrating and living in the ways the Author of life designed. We are the salt and light of the world [Matthew 5: 14]. When the light exposes darkness, there is bound to be a reaction. We refuse to be beaten into submission. When the Church does not address these things, the outcome will always be the same—the world, speedily gravitating to a lost eternity.

I am sure you agree with me: If you purchased a car [an automobile] and wished that it would turn into an aeroplane by taking it to an airport runway, you could never fly that car, regardless of how fast you drove it. Similarly, there is no other acceptable form of marriage in God's eyes. There are Canaanites [unbeliever], and then there are children of God [Church]. Which one are you? If you are a child of God, you will do as He commands—not out of duty or coercion but because you want to. You shall not intermarry with them [the unbeliever], giving your daughters to their sons or taking their daughters for your sons, for they would turn away your sons from following me, to serve other gods. Then the anger of the Lord would be kindled against you, and He would destroy you quickly [Deuteronomy 7: 3 - 4].

A prominent Bible example is Solomon who loved many foreign women, along with the daughter of Pharaoh; Moabite, Ammonite, Edomite, Sidonian, and Hittite women, from the nations concerning which the Lord had said to the people of Israel, "You shall not enter into marriage with them, neither they with you, for surely, they will turn away your heart after their gods." Despite his wisdom, and God's warning, Solomon clung to these foreign women. He had 700 wives, who were princesses, and 300 concubines, and his wives turned away his heart. For when Solomon was old, his wives turned away his heart after their gods, and his heart was not wholly true to the Lord his God, as was the heart of David his father [I Kings 11: 1 - 4]. Do not be equally yoked with an unbeliever, no matter how attractive or beautiful. Their lips drip honey [Proverbs 5: 3] and will lead you away from God. Remember, the Old Testament is a shadow of the New Testament. Here is a story of how we can take a lessons. It is a warning for believers to stay away from ungodly relationships. It is from the Book of Numbers 25: 1 – 2; 5 - 8:

While the Israelites were camped at Acacia, some of the men defiled themselves by sleeping with the local Moabite women. These women invited them to attend sacrifices to their gods, and soon the Israelites were feasting with them and worshiping the gods of Moab. So, Moses ordered Israel's judges to kill everyone who had [yoked and intertwined with the Moabite women] and joined in worshiping Baal of Peor. Behold one of the Israel men came and brought a Midianite woman to his family, in the sight of Moses and in the sight of the whole congregation of the people of Israel while they were weeping in the entrance of the tent of meeting. When Phinehas, son of Eleazar and grandson of Aaron the priest, saw this, he jumped up and left the assembly. Then he took a spear and rushed after the man into his tent. Phinehas thrust the spear all the way through the man's body and into the woman's stomach. Therefore, the plague against the Israelites was stopped.

If there is blood and guts as a consequence of an unholy alliance in the Old Testament, what is the result in our day [New Testament]? Let us be ruthlessly honest and transparent about this; there is no middle of the road practice or consideration. For every Isaac, there is a Rebekah, and for every prince, there is a princess. If you desire marriage, you will meet someone. He cares about every minute detail of your life.

I have also grown to appreciate how God is full of humour and surprises and how He allows us to walk through certain seasons in life, so that we totally become reliant on Him alone. When I was born again in the city of Bulawayo, 26 September 1996, I was involved in a vibrant young adults' group, which was full of young men. Most of the young men were both naturally and spiritually more mature and more gifted than I was. Some were already eloquent preachers, and some mightily used in the gifts of the Spirit while others were teachers of the Word. Still, others were called into the ministry whilst some were yet in their infancy of being successful in business. Coupled with this were many young single beautiful sisters in the Church. I was just beginning my walk with God and just starting a career in the mining industry, as a metallurgist. I was so focussed that I told God that if I were to marry, He would need to confirm this to my future spouse and me. In fact, because I had no girls coming home, my dad was concerned that there was something wrong with me. Clearly, the way my wife and I married was God led. I worked and lived in a remote mine in a relatively small community far away from the city and I did not have any distractions. My routine was very simple; I went to work, came home where I lived alone, and spent time with God.

One of the ways God speaks to me is by dreams and visions [Genesis 37: 5, Numbers 12: 6, Deuteronomy 13: 1 & Matthew 2: 12]. When I had a dream about a particular young lady in the Church, I was certain that I had heard from God. In eagerness, I approached her and went out with her a couple of times for meals. We certainly talked and laughed. At the time, I liked her and thought we were good for each other. I also thought she liked me too, but I did not formally ask her for courtship.

I guess I should have known sooner what to do, but I guess I had to go through some things to be able to teach others. After all, we are a sum total of our experiences. The first red flag was that in private, she seemed to enjoy my company, however in public, and especially when our pastor was around, she was different – perhaps even embarrassed of me. It was also during that time that I also began to fully grasp what Jesus meant when He said, 'Whoever acknowledges me before others, I will also acknowledge before my Father in Heaven, but whoever denies me before others, I will also deny before my Father in Heaven' [Matthew 10: 32 – 33]. Just as our relationship with Jesus is not just private, it must be for all to see and know; if anyone is embarrassed or shy of you in public, they do not deserve you. In hindsight, I should have walked away immediately, but I did not.

On one occasion, I had another dream; God showed me that the same young lady was in a sexual relationship with a man I had never seen before. I did not tell her or feel it was my place to question her. After all, she had been born again longer than me, probably years before me. Who was I to challenge her? The whole experience pained me. Upon reflection, God had warned me in the dream, telling me to move on, but once again, I followed my flesh and mind. One day when I visited her, she introduced me to the man from my dream [in the flesh, prior to that moment, I had never seen him]. When we parted company, I left them together, went home, and wept before God. I confessed that I had not listened to Him and asked for forgiveness. My pursuit of this young lady immediately stopped.

Several months later after the painful incident and having emotionally disconnected from the young lady, I had another dream. In my dream I was clearly in a worship gathering. Suddenly a beautiful young lady who had been leading the worship approached and sat next to me. She lay her left hand over my right hand, and said, "Don't worry, my dear; I am right here." Being a young bachelor, living alone on a mine, I immediately woke up and thanked God. I did not know who she was and did not start searching as I knew that the matter had been settled in Heaven—my wife was waiting for me. I fell asleep again and had another dream. This time I was in a car, with my pastor driving, and his wife seated in the front passenger next to him. I was seated directly behind my pastor, and as I turned to my left, there was this beautiful young lady. Once again, she held my hand as if to assure me that she was there for me. It took me a while to understand that God had allowed me to have a glimpse into the future, so that I did not panic. When I got that revelation, from that day onwards, I decided to be like Job:

I made a covenant with my eyes not to look with lust at a young woman Job 31: 1

After I had made this *agreement* with God, every time I was back in the city on a short break from work on the mine, it was as though either the light in me was turned on, or there were suddenly many young ladies wanting to be around me. It took much discipline and wisdom to politely fend potential alliances that would have derailed me from God's best for me.

Approximately three years after my dream, I was visiting my two best friends in the city, when I met a beautiful young lady [who is now my wife]. I immediately knew in my spirit that this was the lady God had shown me in my dreams. It frightened and excited me at the same time. As we got more acquainted, I later found out that she was in the worship team of her local church. My mind almost discouraged me as I remembered my previous experiences. When I further realised that there were many other suitors, most of them materially worth more than me, I almost threw in the towel. However, thank God for the Holy Spirit who led me. He encouraged me through the Word. The Holy Spirit reminded me of the children of Israel and the occupied promise land [Exodus 3: 17]. I began to understand that sometimes, God gives you a promise, but you will have to walk by faith, not by sight; standing and watching Him defeat nations or giants, so that when the dream comes to fruition, no man, except God receives the glory! She is still worth it. I am glad she picked me—we were happily married in 2001, and she has made me the happiest man on earth. We need to encourage the generations never to compromise and never to marry outside of God's direction but to follow Him, precept upon precept. I believe God is speaking, even to you.

When God was leading the Children of Israel back from exile after having previously been overrun by the Babylonians, amongst the group of those returning was Ezra, who agonised when he saw the detestable intermarriages that were taking place:

Ezra 9: 1 - 11 (ESV)
*"After these things had been done, the officials approached me and said, 'The **people of Israel and the priests and the Levites have not separated themselves from the peoples of the lands** with their abominations, from the Canaanites, the Hittites, the Perizzites, the Jebusites, the Ammonites, the Moabites, the Egyptians, and the Amorites. **For they have taken some of their daughters to be wives***

for themselves and their sons, so that the holy race has mixed itself with the peoples of the lands. And in this faithlessness, the hand of the officials and chief men has been foremost.' As soon as I heard this, I tore my garment and my cloak and pulled hair from my head and beard and sat appalled. Then all who trembled at the words of the God of Israel, because of the faithlessness of the returned exiles, gathered around me while I sat appalled until the evening sacrifice. And at the evening sacrifice, I rose from my fasting, with my garment and my cloak torn, and fell upon my knees and spread out my hands to the Lord my God, saying: 'O my God, I am ashamed and blush to lift my face to you, my God, for our iniquities have risen higher than our heads, and our guilt has mounted up to the heavens. From the days of our fathers to this day we have been in great guilt. And for our iniquities we, our kings, and our priests have been given into the hand of the kings of the lands, to the sword, to captivity, to plundering, and to utter shame, as it is today. But now for a brief moment favour has been shown by the Lord our God, to leave us a remnant and to give us a secure hold within his holy place, that our God may brighten our eyes and grant us a little reviving in our slavery. For we are slaves. Our God has not forsaken us in our bondage but has extended to us his steadfast love before the kings of Persia, to grant us some reviving to set up the house of our God, to repair its ruins, and to give us protection in Judea and Jerusalem. "And now, O our God, what shall we say after this? For we have forsaken your commandments, which you commanded by your servants the prophets, saying, 'The land that you are entering, to take possession of it, is a land impure with the impurity of the peoples of the lands, with their abominations that have filled it from end to end with their uncleanness. Therefore, do not give your daughters to their sons, neither take their daughters for your sons, and never seek their peace or prosperity, that you may be strong and eat the good of the land and leave it for an inheritance to your children forever.' And after all, that has come upon us for our evil deeds and our great guilt, seeing that you, our God, have punished us less than our iniquities deserved and have given us such a remnant as this, shall we break your commandments again and intermarry with the peoples who practice these abominations? Would you not be angry with us until you consumed us so that there should be no remnant, nor any to escape? O Lord, the God of Israel, you are just, for we are left a remnant that has escaped as it is today. Behold, we are before you in our guilt, for none can stand before you because of this."

We must urge the coming generations not to intermarry with the world and be unequally yoked with unbelievers. What harmony is there between Christ and Belial? What does a believer have in common with an unbeliever [II Corinthians 6: 15]? We should given no room to denominationalism. Just as we see in plants, any one group caught up in itself [without cross pollination], will result in an inherent weakness down the line.

COVENANT: MENTORSHIP

A Mentor is someone who imparts wisdom and shares knowledge with a less experienced colleague. Merriam-Webster's Dictionary defines Mentor as someone who teaches or gives help and advice to a less experienced and often younger person. Some outstanding mentors in the Bible were Caleb, David, Mordecai, and Naomi. We rarely hear these characters portrayed as mentors, but I would like to take time and applaud these four characters.

HADASSAH - GROWING UP IN THE HOUSE OF MORDECAI

Esther 2: 5-7 & 19, 20 (NIV)
5 – 7: Now there was in the citadel of Susa a Jew of the tribe of Benjamin, named Mordecai, son of Jair, the son of Shimei, the son of Kish, who had been carried into exile from Jerusalem by Nebuchadnezzar king of Babylon, among those taken captive with Jehoiachin king of Judah. Mordecai had a cousin named Hadassah, whom he had brought up because she had neither father nor mother. This young woman, who was also known as Esther, had a lovely

*figure and was beautiful. **Mordecai had taken her as his daughter
when her father and mother died.***

*19 & 20: When the virgins were assembled a second time, Mordecai
was sitting at the king's gate.* ***But Esther had kept secret her family
background and nationality just as Mordecai had told her to do, for
she continued to follow Mordecai's instructions as she had done
when he was bringing her up.***

Hadassah was an orphan. Her story would have been written off had
she lived in our day. In a modern British Society, she would probably
have been a social service case, perhaps even viewed as a state child.
At some point in her life, in the same society, as an adult she may have
gravitated towards unemployment and living on benefit claims. On
the flipside, had she lived in most modern-day societies, she would
have died a slow, lonely death. It is highly unlikely that she would
have been that fortunate. She may have died of starvation, with no
one to take care of her. But thank God there are people like Mordecai.
People who re-define family, stretch out into uncharted territory,
and change history for those who would have otherwise been labelled
failures. In Mordecai, I see a man who was unsatisfied; I sense a holy
discontent and a passionate man pursuing continuity.

Mordecai chose to adopt and look after his father's brother's [his
uncle's] daughter, Hadassah. He took her into his home, to love her as
if she were his daughter, to teach and protect her. He was not forced,
blackmailed, or even manipulated to do so. What he did was quite
extraordinary. Here are some thoughts: Did Jair [Mordecai's father]
not have any other brothers or sisters who were still alive to look
after their nephew? On the other hand, did Hadassah's late mother
not have siblings who were alive and prepared to take care of her?
Was Hadassah an only child, and did she not have any older siblings
capable of looking after her? When you consider the distance in
Mordecai and Hadassah's blood relationship, you can see that it took
an exceptional person to step forward and do what he did. In my view,

Mordecai was a non-conformist; it is likely that he faced all sorts of reactions head on, both verbal and unspoken.

In Hebrew, Hadassah means myrtle, which is a type of tree. The myrtle wood trees grow slowly and can be identified by their very short, thick trunks. Mordecai must have seen this orphan girl's potential and decided that his mission was not only to teach her but to take her under his wing and influence her. He would father her. Picture this; just as at birth, parents name a child. Mordecai did the same. He stripped the name Hadassah and renamed her Esther. Esther in Hebrew means star and peace. The slowly growing stunted tree became a star. From being an ordinary common child with a chaotic past, Uncle Mordecai ensured that the young lady was brought into a place of refuge and peace and that she be called and identified as, supernaturally ordinary. Every time people would call her by name, they would be reminded of where she stood. She lived in the sky, where stars belong – that she is the head and not the tail, above and not beneath [Deuteronomy 28: 13]. This, in turn, would have shifted her paradigm, elevated her thinking, and ultimately changed her perception of self.

I can picture life lessons being learnt in the house of Mordecai. Esther was not only a good student, but she also lived out what she learnt. She trained herself to obey. The Bible says, "Children obey your parents *in the Lord*, for this is right. Honour your father and mother," which is the first commandment with a promise, so that it may go well with you and that you may enjoy long life on the earth [Ephesians 6: 1 - 3]. Obedience comes from a Greek word "hupakou," which means to listen attentively, and by implication, to heed or conform to a command or authority. This word conveys the idea of actively following a command. There is no choice in the matter; it is to be done whether one agrees with it or not. Obedience is, therefore, involuntary. In this manner, Esther became a doer of the word and not just a hearer.

In Esther, we see a new generation willing to receive and to use the preceding generation's peak as a platform to catapult itself into the future. Verse 20, as quoted above, speaks volumes, and demonstrates the type of person Esther was. Here was a collision, a merging, or a fusion of two generations. The old was imparting to the new, and the new generation openly received instructions. The collision I picture here is not of disorganised chaos. In my mind, I see what Ezekiel saw in the valley of dry bones [chapter 37]. I see phalanges for a particular individual identifying and merging with each other, desperately moving through a mound of other bones in the process of identifying and knitting to themselves.

Specific phalanges finding their specific metatarsals, and these in turn connecting to their specific tibia and fibula. I see a patella jump and join, then the femur, bone after bone connecting all the way through, till a skeleton was fully formed. Following on from this is the sinew, and then a Man arises. You see, in young Esther's mind, attitude, and character, would have initially been a storm, being calmed, being redirected, being refocused, and being re-arranged by Mordecai, and turned into a place of peace and tranquillity. She is told a detailed lesson of her heritage: her true identity and who her Father [God] is. She is told that she is no ordinary young lady but extraordinary. She is reminded of the past victories and informed of the errors and mistakes of the previous generations. Mordecai tells her to watch him and that she should excel beyond him. She is told she is a princess and an heir apparent.

What further echoes in verse 20 is a desire and willingness for a new generation to accept and go further.

DAVID: UPROOTING COMPROMISE

I Kings 2: 1 - 6 (GNT)
When David was about to die, he called his son Solomon and gave him his last instructions: "My time to die has come. Be confident and determined and do what the Lord your God orders you to do.

*Obey all his laws and commands, as written in the Law of Moses, so that wherever you go you may prosper in everything you do. If you obey him, the Lord will keep the promise he made when he told me that my descendants would rule Israel as long as they were careful to follow his commands faithfully with all their heart and soul. "There is something else. You remember what **Joab** did to me by killing the two commanders of Israel's armies, Abner, son of Ner and Amasa, son of Jether. You remember how he murdered them in a time of peace as revenge for deaths they had caused in a time of war. He killed innocent men, and now I bear the responsibility for what he did, and I suffer the consequences. **You know what to do; you must not let him die a natural death**.*

The stories, exploits, and life of David are loved by most. He was a shepherd boy who the prophet Samuel would have missed as God's anointed king—a man after God's heart. David lived his life fully. He experienced much. His walk with God is well documented. He held nothing back. His successes, errors and his mistakes are on display for all to see. He was an inspirational leader and led from the front, yet he was also a murderer, an adulterer, and he compromised. The above verses illustrate an elderly David exposing himself to his son Solomon and clearly highlighting that his compromise should not manifest in the next generation. "Kill Joab!" is what David said. In these last days, God will not tolerate compromise.

I am certain that it was not easy for David; Joab was captain of his army, and the son of Zeruiah, a sister of David [2 Samuel 8:16; 20: 23; 1 Chronicles 11:6; 18:15; 27:34]. Can you imagine killing your own close relative? Earlier in life, David had compromised, probably looked the other way, and let Joab get away with many things; Joab killed Abner who came to reconcile with David [II Samuel 3: 26-30]. He also killed Absalom, third son of David, even though David had given specific instructions for no harm to come to Absalom [II Samuel 18], and Joab also killed Amasa, who had been appointed captain by David [II Samuel 20].

The Bride [the Church] must be presented to the Groom [Jesus], spotless and without blemish. Here is a wise David speaking to his son. These last words of a dying father and king are precious and worthy of note. I picture these words like the last drops in a cup. It is a father pouring out his final counsel. I am reminded of an incident when I was four years old. We travelled as a family to see my father's uncle who had been very ill. Instead of going to play outside, I opted to sit and listen as this old man talked. He knew he was dying; it was just a matter of time. He gave instructions to his children, who were young adults, in their early to mid-twenties. He also made specific requests to my father, on how his family was to run after his death. Throughout scripture, we see several incidences where advice, warning, and encouragement are given by a dying father.

In Joshua 23:1-24:28, when Joshua was very old, he got together with all the people of Israel, their elders, their heads, their judges, and their officers to tell them some very important things. He told the people that he was about to die but reminded the people of how faithful God had been to Israel and how He had taken them out of captivity and brought them to a place of rest. Joshua encouraged the people to love God and not serve any other. For Joshua and his family [descendants], they would serve no other. Then, he said, "I want you to be strong. Do everything that God told you to do. Do not disobey God's commands. Do not turn away from God. Trust Him." And the people said to Joshua, "No, but we will serve the Lord!"

Old man Paul wrote to Timothy too [II Timothy 4]. He knew his time was up. He was in his twilight, and life was beginning to ebb away. He was on the home straight. In verse 6, Paul told Timothy, "For I am already being poured out like a drink offering, and the time for my departure is near." The thought of death did not frighten Paul at all, but, instead, he continued to teach. He urged Timothy to run his race and to finish it. He told Timothy that, in the last days, the people would not put up with sound doctrine.

Instead, to suit their own desires, they will gather a great number of teachers to listen to what their itching ears want to hear, and they will turn their ears away from the truth and turn to the myths. Paul further personalises the letter; he tells Timothy that compromise has entered those who are close; "Demas loved this world and has deserted me and has gone to Thessalonica. Crescens has gone to Galatia, and Titus has gone to Dalmatia." Lastly, Paul warns Timothy not to hang around anywhere near Alexander. "Alexander, the metalworker, did me a great deal of harm. The Lord will repay him for what he has done. You, too, should be on your guard against him because he strongly opposed our message."

There is no room and place for compromise.

NAOMI - TENACITY IN ADVERSITY

Ruth 1: 3-5, 16-18 (NIV)

3 – 5; Now, Elimelek, Naomi's husband, died, and she was left with her two sons. They married Moabite women, one named Orpah and the other Ruth. After they had lived there about ten years, both Mahlon and Kilion also died, and Naomi was left without her two sons and her husband.

16- 18: But Ruth replied, "Don't urge me to leave you or to turn back from you. Where you go, I will go, and where you stay, I will stay. Your people will be my people and your God my God. Where you die, I will die, and there I will be buried. May the Lord deal with me, be it ever so severely, if even death separates you and me." When Naomi realized that Ruth was determined to go with her, she stopped urging her.

Years ago, I was told that a certain situation can cause an adrenalin rush. When we have a run of adrenalin, there are three different reactions for how will we respond—fright, flight, or fight. Adversity requires a response—and if the truth be told, none of us want to go through difficult or tough situations. In the face of adversity, there are two types of people: There is one who will run off and hide, and there is the other who will stay the course. Given the choice, I know which of the two people I would like in my team. Both reactions are not genetically inherited. We cannot excuse our responses down to our genetic makeup or DNA. Both reactions are a direct reflection of the environment we have been exposed to and nurtured in. Our reactions will be a function of lack of training and instruction or a lack of icons and role models. A positive response results in having the ability to stand while a negative response results in a coward-like reaction. Some people will freeze in their tracks because they are rendered immobile with fright or are confused and do not know how to react; alternatively, they will likely take flight, crying. In sharp contrast, when the battle heats up, there are others who will roll up their sleeves and have the tenacity to stay and face their circumstances. They will not flinch; they will grind their teeth and refuse to be deterred. They are not ignorant of what they are going through, but they refuse to wallow.

In the Book of Ruth, there are two young women faced with similar harsh conditions, and both live with a wise old lady, but they react very differently to these conditions. They both have an opportunity to chart their destinies. Naomi, their mother-in-law, is a woman of faith and experience, and we see how after she lost her husband and sons, she unbuckles her seat belt, comes out of her pity party, and chooses to remain God's daughter—to be Naomi, which means beautiful and joyful rather than Mara, which means sorrow [Ruth 1: 20].

Ruth and Orpah married into the same family and lost their husbands. They were both in similar situations, but they responded very differently. This dichotomy is seen everywhere. I could give you numerous examples of people I know, all very close, growing up in the same house, under similar circumstances, but who ended up living very different lives. The sorrowful end of Ruth and Orpah's marriages to Naomi's sons must have been heart wrenching experiences. I can imagine both women in mourning and in need of comfort, and yet their overall reactions are poles apart. Ruth's reaction is clearly documented in detail and forever etched in history. Orpah, on the other hand, appears to make an appearance together with Ruth but ebbs away with no future and no further documented evidence of continuity. Such was the manner of Ruth's response that she bore a royal lineage [Matthew 1: 1 – 16].

The wisdom of Naomi is unveiled in the pages of the Book of Ruth; her heart is revealed, and her motives are understood. Naomi is loving, caring, and honest. She has such experience, knowledge, and wisdom and is willing to impart this to the next generation. She is not your typical mother-in-law or elderly lady who just sits still. She is not easily fazed by what goes on around her. She is selfless and not selfish or cunning. Her world seems to be falling apart; the loss of her husband and her two sons means that there will be three funerals within a short span of time and that there is no male presence in her household. Traditionally, the household income would be brought in by the husband. His absence would mean that the responsibility would fall on the sons. Their subsequent deaths meant that there was no breadwinner in the home. There is a strength that exudes from Naomi. She is not wallowing in self-pity and seeking attention from anyone. She provides surety and steadiness as she communicates with her daughters-in-law. There is composure, well-thought reasoning in her persona. Some mothers-in-law would have exploited the situation and been manipulative. Instead, Naomi urges Ruth and Orpah to move on and restart their lives. She understands that she cannot provide the physical seed for the two ladies to bear children.

Naomi loves her daughters-in-law so much that she is willing to let them go and see them flourish in the future. At the parting of Orpah from Naomi, I can picture an emotional moment; here were three ladies, genuinely crying from their hearts. Orpah made her mind up; she decided to leave, and that is the last we hear from her. Ruth, on the other hand, had a tugging in her heart; she could not tell the end from the beginning, and it probably did not make sense at the time she made her decision, but she stayed. She had the tenacity to stay. Contrary to the circumstances she was in, she wept with determination not to leave this precious elderly woman she now probably called mom.

Do you remember Jacob wrestling with God in Genesis 32: 22 - 30? Even though Jacob sensed he was wrestling with a heavenly being and that he was unlikely to overcome such a creature, he did not throw in the towel. Naturally, he knew that he could have been blown away; he, instead, grit his teeth and clung on for life. They wrestled until it was near daybreak. This was not a quick three-minute match. Imagine the exhaustion, the sweat, the blood, and the dislocation of the hip—Jacob still persevered. He probably dug his fingers in the belt of the heavenly being and then locked his legs. Ordinarily, Jacob should have been a goner, but he defied all odds; he was tenacious, sagacious, and bold. God changed Jacob's life from here on. We know that God changed his name and, effectively, the man himself. The rest is history. In my imagination, I believe that this was a similar wrestling in the heart and mind that Ruth underwent. Just as Israel declared in verse 30 of chapter 32 of the book of Genesis, it is because I saw God face to face, and yet my life was spared. Ruth confidently declared this:

Ruth 1: 16 - 17 (ESV)
But Ruth said, "Do not urge me to leave you or to return from following you. For where you go, I will go, and where you lodge, I will lodge. Your people shall be my people, and your God my God. Where you die, I will die, and there will I be buried. May the Lord do so to me and more also if anything but death parts me from you."

CALEB: PATIENT MANIFESTATION OF GOD'S WORD

Joshua 14:6 - 14 (KJV)
*Then the children of Judah came unto Joshua in Gilgal: and Caleb the son of Jephunneh the Kenezite said unto him, thou knowest the thing that **the Lord said unto Moses the man of God concerning me and thee** in Kadeshbarnea. **Forty years old was I when Moses the servant of the Lord sent me from Kadeshbarnea to espy out the land;** and I brought*

him word again as it was in mine heart. Nevertheless my brethren that went up with me made the heart of the people melt: but I wholly followed the Lord my God and Moses sware on that day, saying, surely the land whereon thy feet have trodden shall be thine inheritance, and thy children's forever, because thou hast wholly followed the Lord my God and now, behold, **the Lord hath kept me alive, as he said, these forty and five years, even since the Lord spake this word unto Moses,** *while the children of Israel wandered in the wilderness: and* **now, lo, I am this day fourscore and five years old. As yet I am as strong this day as I was in the day that Moses sent me: as my strength was then, even so is my strength now, for war, both to go out, and to come in. Now therefore give me this mountain, whereof the Lord spake in that day;** *for thou heardest in that day how the Anakims were there, and that the cities were great and fenced: if so be the Lord will be with me, then I shall be able to drive them out, as the Lord said. And Joshua blessed him and gave unto Caleb the son of Jephunneh Hebron for an inheritance. Hebron therefore became the inheritance of Caleb the son of Jephunneh the Kenezite unto this day because that he wholly followed the Lord God of Israel.*

Caleb had a different spirit; he followed God wholeheartedly [Numbers 14: 24]. Of the population of no less than six hundred thousand men [Exodus 12: 3], only Caleb and Joshua would enter the promise land. Caleb was forty years old when he received the promise from God. One by one, the unbelieving and rebellious generation died. I can picture, with each death, Joshua and Caleb counting down the numbers as that generation dwindled. Can you imagine the last one of that generation, hoping that God would change His mind and spare their life, just to catch a glimpse of the promise land? To that older generation, Joshua and Caleb would have been living monuments. They served as daily reminders of what could have been and where they would have gone. As they say, so near, yet so far. Some would have been thinking, "If only at the time I had decided to have a better attitude, I would have made it to the promised land." With each new birth in each tribe, frantic effort was being made by each parent and relative, urging the next generation to be patient, wholeheartedly follow God, and follow the example of Joshua and Caleb. Their impatience and lack of faith and trust in God would be told to the new generation. Such was the impact of the dying generation that the new generation was remarkable. The scripture that sums it up is as follows:

Joshua 1:16-18 *(ESV)*

And they answered Joshua, "All that you have commanded us we will do, and wherever you send us we will go. Just as we obeyed Moses in all things, so we will obey you. Only may the Lord your God be with you, as he was with Moses! Whoever rebels against your commandment and disobeys your words, whatever you command him, shall be put to death. Only be strong and courageous."

To Joshua, this new generation said, "We will do as commanded, we will go as you send, we will fully obey, and we will kill whoever is against your word and does not obey."

As Joshua led in the forefront, in the background, fully obedient and exemplary, would have been the now elder statesman, Caleb, still full of vigour, vitality and the energy of youth. He was Joshua's echo, speaking and demonstrating the very same things. In the eyes of the young generation, Caleb would have been a pillar of strength. Here was an old man who had seen it all, right from childhood— the plagues in Egypt, the manna from Heaven, water from a rock, crossing the Red Sea and the waters parting, the water instantly freezing, and walking on a dry seabed. He not only told the stories, but he also recounted them as if they had happened yesterday. He was there in the flesh when it all happened.

In Joshua Chapter 14, 45 years after the promise, Caleb reminds Joshua of God's promise to him. Those in hearing range would have been astounded as Caleb was now 85 years old and still going strong. He was calling or speaking those things that are not as though they are—simply put, that is faith! The name Caleb is thought to have originated from the word kelev meaning dog. From the components of that word, 'kal' and 'lev.' In Hebrew Caleb also means wholehearted faith. Whether you want to associate him with a dog or faith and devotion, he was altogether different! Caleb began to understand that God operates in seasons, Kairos, which is the right, supreme or opportune moment and that He does not operate on man's time, Chronos, which is the personification of determinate time. Just as the sons of Issachar [I Chronicles 12:32], Caleb interpreted the season he was entering. Nobody in this generation contemplated giving up. He was an inspiration and a role model and received his promise. However, when Caleb, Joshua, and the generation they led died, we see how that very same generation failed to influence and hand the baton to their children.

Judges 2:8-11 (KJV)

And Joshua, the son of Nun, the servant of the Lord, died, being a hundred and ten years old, and they buried him in the border of his inheritance in Timnathheres, in the mount of Ephraim, on the north side of the hill Gaash and, also, all that generation were gathered unto their fathers; and there arose another generation after them, which knew not the Lord nor yet the works which he had done for Israel and, the children of Israel did evil in the sight of the Lord and served Baalim

Can you imagine John the Baptist hearing the voice of God telling Him to go into the wilderness to prepare the way for the Messiah? For hundreds of years the voice of the Lord had been scarce, and John would have read Isaiah's prophecy [Isaiah 40: 3], recorded hundreds of years earlier. The Word of God endured until it found the right candidate; it did not return to God void, but instead, it accomplished everything it was purposed for. John would have had to interpret the times and then step into the rhema word of God. Also consider Jesus, 100% God because He was conceived by the Holy Spirit, and 100% Man because He was born to Mary; He left His glory and splendour, stepped out of eternity and into time to fulfil the Father's plan. Jesus waited patiently for 30 years before He told the world who He was.

Have you ever come across people who have the call of God on their lives but are impatient? They run off ahead of God before they are ready. In their immature state, they hurt others, short circuit their day of manifestation and elongate their date of commencement. I have known several who either died prematurely or gave up their walk with God in frustration. In those 30 years, every time someone called Jesus by name, can you imagine how He felt? They were literally reminding Him that He is God with us. He could have been tempted to open His mouth and tell the world who He was but didn't. I am reminded that the Bible says that He faced all temptation but overcame [Hebrews 4: 15]. He could have also summoned the angels of God, and they would have come, but He didn't [Matthew 26: 53]. Instead, for 30 years, Jesus was a son of a carpenter, lowly, humble, and lived in obscurity. However, when the day of fulfilment came [Luke 4: 18], He had clearly heard from the Father [John 5: 19] and acted upon it. It took Him 3 years to permanently turn the world upside down, and this will never stop.

We need to stand firm and be patient—walking by faith and not by sight or feelings. When we practice patience, God will always come through for us.

DAVID: STEWARDSHIP OF SUBSTANCE

Deuteronomy 8: 18
But you shall [earnestly] remember the Lord your God, for it is He who gives you the power to get wealth, that He may establish His covenant which He swore to your fathers as it is this day.

I Timothy 6: 17 -18
Command those who are rich in this present world not to be arrogant nor to put their hope in wealth, which is so uncertain, but to put

their hope in God, who richly provides us with everything for our enjoyment.

Just in case you were never told or unaware, everything we have is owned by God. I have highlighted the above verses for emphasis; however, can I encourage you to read Deuteronomy 8: 6 -17. Wealth [or substance] you get by dishonesty will do you no good. The Lord protects honest people but destroys those who do wrong. The dishonest will eventually be caught, but honest people are safe and secure. So, be an honest person. Be sensible, accept good advice, and remember that it is the Lord's blessing that makes you wealthy.

Stewardship is being responsible for something by being fruitful, productive, and protecting what you have been given. The Bible says that it is required [as essential and demanded] of stewards that one be found faithful and trustworthy [I Corinthians 4: 2b]. All of us have been endowed with a gift from God—for example the ability to cut hair, cook, work in administration, teach or mine. For John Roebling, his talent was training up his son, having a dream and vision, making it plain and designing the Brooklyn Bridge, constructing the bridge, and it is still erect and in use after 133 years. For Sir Christopher Wren, it was being obedient to his father, taking on the attitude of continuity and keeping his talent on an open hand and allowing others to complete his architectural design. Because of exercising his gift and allowing it to flow through his hands, St Paul's Cathedral in London is still looking grand, over 650 years later. What sets you apart from the rest? Will you hold onto your precious plans, vision, business ideas, cash, property, die, and be buried with them, or will you leave it for the kingdom and usher in younger generations who will put thousands to flight? We need to impart to the next generation who will speak the word of the Lord saying, 'This is the way, walk in it, and follow us as we follow Christ.'

None of us has the excuse of not having received an ability from God. Invariably, people earn an income, money, or acquire assets using these gifts. The responsibility and accountability of what we do with talent lies with us. Some people pervert their gift, focusing on self, stardom and glory or praise of Man. There are others who recognise the importance of what they have and are kingdom minded, resulting in everyone around them benefiting from the exercised gift. They understand and see clearly that everything belongs to God. They steward because what they have is not their own but belongs to Him. You are responsible for your own actions.

Responsibility is something that you should do because it is morally right or legally required. As believers who are called and walking according to His purpose, I am convinced that God has our best interest at heart and will always ensure our needs are met. However, we need to straighten our understanding of *needs* and *wants*. Years ago, when I studied management, I learned the difference. *Needs* are necessities, such as love, food, water, health, clothing, and shelter, whereas *wants* are desires. We may sometimes want things that we do not need. Therefore, when we repeat scriptures such as, "God shall supply all my *needs* according to His riches in glory in Christ Jesus" [Philippians 4: 19] or "Whatsoever things you *desire*, when you pray, believe that you receive them, and you shall have them" [Mark 11: 24]. Let us firstly understand that our needs and desires line up with the Word and more importantly, not lose heart when God does not necessarily give us our *wants*. The reality is that what belongs to God is ours since we are His sons. Romans 8: 17 reminds us that we are joint heirs with Christ and that we will suffer with Him too. The sufferings are persecutions, including the alternate—to experience pain [not having the substance you want].

Having wealth and owning assets predates our time and is evidenced in the Bible. Our covenant [New Testament Church] with God is built on better promises than those in the Old Testament. To understand wealth and property, you need to consider the birth right from the Old Testament and kingdom principles from the New Testament. In Biblical times, birth right referred to the inheritance rights of the firstborn son in a Hebrew family. Assets from the father were divided among the sons, but the firstborn received a double portion. These privileges and responsibilities could be forfeited through bad behaviour or even stolen by younger brothers. Jesus is the firstborn of all creation [Colossians 1: 15]. We, therefore, share in both the sufferings of Christ and His blessings.

In the parable of the Talents [Matthew 25:14-30], it is clear that we must be good stewards. When Jesus returns, He will require capital [what He gave us] plus the interest [the surplus we made]. We will all have to give an account to God, the One who entrusts us with the talents. It is also clear from the parable that when you have the gift of God, people around you or communities will be affected. The two servants who acted wisely invested and traded to double what they were each entrusted with. To invest is to make use of, for future benefits or advantages. It goes beyond money; it is to commit something in order to earn a return. For example, if you understand the cycle or flow of money, you will understand that these individuals could not have doubled their money without the participation of others. They were inclusive in their actions. Others rode on the crest of their achievements. They directly impacted others, and others would have money too.

You see, trading and investing is very demanding; you put in time and effort, and nothing is handed to you on a silver plate. Their focus was not on the talent. Their goal was to please their Master, and therefore with us we, must use the talents to the glory of God. In their quest to please God, they affected others around them positively. Those affected would have been their own families, directly as well as their trading partners and their families, indirectly. Our talents must be for us, our families and those who we carry a representative responsibility over. The irresponsible servant from the parable focused on self. He was exclusive, a lone wolf, a loner, and one who was interested in self-preservation. Everything centred around himself; he was so caught up on self that he took the eyes off his Master. He chose to dig a hole and hide the talent. It is clear to me that as this servant hid the talent, he would have visited it time and time again, to ensure that it was safe. No one knew he even had a talent, and no one benefited from his talent. This servant is no different to people who want to be idolised, placed on a pedestal as the only ones who can do this or that. They are caught up in image or status—it is about self. In their hearts, they want to receive the glory and praise of Man, that is why the servant said, 'You are a hard man, reaping where you did not sow, and gathering where you scattered no seed, so I was afraid, and I went and hid your talent in the ground. Here, you have what is yours.' Let us not be found wanting or fall short—God is not mocked; we will be weighed. Let us come out of this Litmus Test, pure and clean. Let us obey His word.

Obedience and walking with God also means that He supplies all our needs, exceeds all our expectations, and will sometimes give us in abundance so that we, in turn, affect and bless others. The Bible says that Isaac became rich and continued to grow richer until he became very wealthy, for he had possessions of flocks and herds and a great household [Genesis 26: 13]. Of Jacob, the Bible says that he became exceedingly prosperous and had large flocks and female and male servants and camels and donkeys. Also, Joseph became a very wealthy man while in the house of his Egyptian master.

As believers, the first thing we need to realise where possessions are concerned, is that it is God who gives us the right, the permission, the authority, and the ability to obtain wealth, property, or assets. It is true that we have been endowed with gifts that make room for us [Proverbs 18: 16], but ultimately, it is God who gives us the power to acquire wealth. When the Church talks about money, I often see people get uncomfortable, but if we do not talk about it, then who should? We use currency every day, so let's talk about how to handle it and not be a slave to it. Let us remember that Jesus is still the Lord, and we are the citizens of His kingdom, living, submitting to, and loving His principles. We worship no other gods, not even mammon. I have seen a lot of hype and excesses in some church denomination teachings on prosperity—from miracle money to some absurd calls which are manipulation, coercion, and extortion, supposedly tied to God's blessing. What I have learned is this: If it is not in God's Word, do not ascribe.

Prosperity means more than money or assets. The Bible shows us that God is loving and relational, and not an automated teller machine ("ATM") for you to just draw money as you feel like it. Frighteningly, one day we will all stand before God and give an account of what we have said and done. Given some of the excesses that are prevalent in some church denominations, the flip side is that the world does not like to see financially sound and asset-rich Christians, who genuinely walk with God. Instead, they want all Christians to be financially and asset poor. Sadly, in both cases, the excesses, and the world's ignorance and misinterpretation of the Bible, have completely challenged the Body of Christ's position.

The truth is that oil and water are immiscible, and light and darkness have nothing in common. However, the Church needs to be that light which glows and leads people [the world] to Christ, which is our primary mandate, and we are also to stay consistently in the Word. The longer I have walked with God, the more I have learnt how important it is to always to go back to Scripture and to see what it says, just as the Bereans did in Acts 17:11. We have too many eloquent speakers nowadays, whose lips drip honey, and are in fact teaching very grey areas. Even as you read this book, check things out for yourself and make sure you are on the correct side of the road.

Wealth is the value of the property, the possessions, and the money that a person has. The quantity can be a meagre or a significant amount of money or plenty of assets. It can also be an abundance of valuable resources. The degree to which we each find satisfaction and fulfilment regarding money and property is always relative. Each of us has a starting point; we all have a measure of wealth, and some have more than others. However, we are all expected to handle what we have responsibly. We are supposed to start with the little we have, grow, and increase it for the benefit of others, and primarily God's kingdom. As stated before, in the parable of the Talents (Matthew 25: 14 - 30), this is very clear.

It seems that in the original DNA of the Church [Acts 2: 44 - 45], the sharing and transferring of possessions was normal. There was nothing unique about such practices—it was natural, ordinary, and not done to gain man's approval or affirmation, and neither was it done to grow in recognition and status. Those in need did not suffer because those living in abundance shared. The picture painted here is not of one-off gifts, it is not of a Church beggar sitting at the door asking for alms and another pulling out a couple of coins from his pocket. This is not to say that there were no beggars at all as this would be an insult to the Word of God.

In Acts 3, Peter and John did see a man asking for alms, and they met his need. They gave him what they had—they gave him Jesus! This transformation of the beggar was both in natural as it meant that he became able-bodied and spiritual in that he would spend eternity with Jesus. In imagining the early Church, I see those with investment portfolios cashing them in to ensure needs were met. Remember Zacchaeus, Luke 19? Definitive action resulting in a permanent, sustainable, established solution. Such people are those whom Jesus described in Matthew 25: 35: "For I was hungry, and you fed me. I was thirsty, and you gave me a drink. I was a stranger, and you invited me into your home."

Jesus also talked about how to handle money and possessions on numerous occasions. In fact, more than ten parables relate to money. Owning wealth and possessions is not evil. Ecclesiastes 10: 19b says money answers all things. Talking about how to create greater wealth and leave an inheritance [money, property, and assets] is not forbidden. We need to know how to handle money and possessions and that these possessions and things are not the ones controlling us. I am not advocating that we amass wealth and fill our pockets before we die because according to I Timothy 6: 10, the love of money is the root of all evil. We all need to understand that we have the choice to give or to withhold. I believe that giving a portion and pretending that we are giving in full will result in death. Ananias and Sapphira [Acts 5] lied, and God killed them, and continuity ceased because of the love of money. Everything we do is not for the show; I encourage people to act responsibly with what they have and teach the coming generations to go further, grow incrementally, and pass on or transfer wealth.

A good man leaves an inheritance to his children's children, and the wealth of the unjust is laid up for the righteous [Proverbs 13: 22]. One of the reasons behind the existence of poverty in the world is that much of the wealth is in the wrong hands. I once read an article by one of the richest men in the world, whose aim and desire is to eradicate poverty; honestly, he will fail to achieve this. God alone will eradicate poverty, in the new earth [Revelation 21]. The world thrives on riding on one class or group of people. Look at every area in the world, from foodstuffs, clothing and shelter. Someone is being taken advantage of. Am I saying this wealthy man should give up on his aim and wait to die? Certainly not. Let him do as he pleases with his money. It is only through the Church [Body of Christ] that he would make a significant or greater impact.

MOVE, SHIFT, & TRANSMIT

As mentioned before, the early Church shared their possessions [Acts 2: 44 - 45]. Tithing and generous giving was passed down through the generations, predating the Law. Abel brought his first fruits to God [Genesis 4: 4 and Proverbs 3: 9], and Abraham tithed to Melchizedek [Genesis 14 and Hebrews 7]. The Bible clearly reminds that we ought to give cheerfully, for that is the person God loves. Jesus commended the woman who gave the little she had [Luke 21: 1 - 4]. It is not in the measure of how much you give; it is about obeying the principle and giving whole-heartedly. We are not to give reluctantly or under compulsion [II Corinthians 9: 6 - 7].

Another woman had invested her finance in perfume. She had perfume, which was the value of 1 year's income, but she did not hold back—she poured it on Jesus—that is unorthodox! [John 12: 5]. I believe that the tithe should be what we pay first, without hesitancy or compromise, and it must be based on our income. The 90% goes a lot further as God blesses it. It goes further than the 100% that we may deceitfully hold onto as it is cursed and is temporary. As full citizens of the Kingdom of God, when we have wealth, it means that there is wealth in the Kingdom.

When connected to God and walking with Him, Man will live an abundant and supernatural life. In Him [God, through His Son Jesus], we live, move, and have our being (Acts 17: 28). In Acts 2: 44 - 45, we read that 'all those who had believed in Jesus Christ were together and had all things in common; and they began selling their property and possessions and were *sharing* them with all as anyone might have needed.' A simple fact is that you cannot or should not sell what you do not have, and you do not share, if there is not going to be a portion of the allocation left for you. Assets and money were being shared and transferred amongst the believers.

I remember that there were things that David did in his day, which even in our day, would blow people's minds. We are told that the Old Testament is 'a shadow' of our time; 'The old system under the law of Moses was only a shadow, a dim preview of the good things to come [which are the current times we live in]. I am sure David read the Book of Exodus, Chapters 35 & 36, and saw what Moses did when he wanted to build the Tabernacle [and David desired that God live in a Temple—the next level]; when he was at a good old age, David summoned the hierarchy of Israel and spoke of his desire to build a house for God. God told him that he was not the one to build the house because he had been a man of war and had shed blood [I Chronicles 28: 3].

I Chronicles 28: 11 - 19 (KJV)

Then David gave to Solomon, his son, the pattern of the porch, and of the houses thereof, and of the treasuries thereof, and of the upper chambers thereof, and of the inner parlours thereof, and of the place of the mercy seat, And the pattern of all that he had by the spirit, of the courts of the house of the LORD, and of all the chambers round about, of the treasuries of the house of God, and of the treasuries of the dedicated things: Also for the courses of the priests and the Levites, and for all the work of the service of the house of the LORD, and for all the vessels of service in the house of the LORD. He gave of gold by weight for things of gold, for all instruments of all manner of service; silver also for all instruments of silver by weight, for all instruments of every kind of service: Even the weight for the candlesticks of gold, and for their lamps of gold, by weight for every candlestick, and for the lamps thereof: and for the candlesticks of silver by weight, both for the candlestick, and also for the lamps thereof, according to the use of every candlestick. And by weight he gave gold for the tables of shewbread, for every table; and likewise silver for the tables of silver: Also, pure gold for the fleshhooks, and the bowls, and the cups: and for the golden basons he gave gold by weight for every bason; and likewise silver by weight for every bason of silver: And for the altar of incense refined gold by weight; and gold for the pattern of the chariot of the cherubims that spread out their wings and covered the ark of the covenant of the LORD. All this said David, the LORD made me understand in writing by his hand upon me, even all the works of this pattern.

David saw the house of the Lord, its dimensions and detail in the spirit [verse 12 and 19]. Just like in my earlier illustration of the story of the construction of the Brooklyn Bridge, David had the first-hand revelation of the temple and passed the full design and picture to his son. He wrote the vision down and made it plain [Habakkuk 2: 2 - 3], and the one who read it and ran with it was Solomon. Solomon experienced the physical or tangible manifestation, and his father, David, experienced the spiritual reality. Spiritual things are real, and they are tangible; David gave the design, the layout, precise measurements, and weights, and even minute details of God's house. In the spirit, David walked into and around the temple. He knew what it looked like. His experience and encounter were as real as Solomon's. What could have been a daunting and arduous task for Solomon turned out to be a productive and favourable twenty years building the temple.

While David's physical body was showing signs of tiredness, his life seemingly slowly ebbing away; his spirit was showing sharpness, alertness, and a desire to finish well. David had prepared for this moment, the day he would unveil what God showed him in private. He was also about to do another thing that others before him had failed to do. Using modern-day language and for the sake of clarity, David "cashed his stocks and shares. He exited from investments and realised the money, as well as amalgamated all his cash and interest"— in preparation for his son Solomon to make the instructions of God into a reality.

Wherever possible, make every effort to arrange financial provision for the next generation. David gave Solomon hundreds of metric tonnes of gold and hundreds of metric tonnes of silver. Swindling is not how he acquired the wealth, and neither was it from over-taxing the people. Clearly, the nation of Israel was prosperous too—see how the people responded to David's actions [I Chronicles 29]. When Israel saw his heart, they were moved and gave willingly and joyfully. Combined, the nation of Israel gave even more than David had given.

I Chronicles 29: 6 - 9 (NLT)
Then, the family leaders, the leaders of the tribes of Israel, the generals and captains of the army, and the king's administrative officers all gave willingly. For the construction of the Temple of God, they gave about 188 tonnes of gold, 10,000 gold coins, 375 tonnes of silver, 675 tonnes of bronze, and 3,750 tonnes of iron. They also contributed numerous precious stones, which were deposited in the treasury of the house of the Lord under the care of Jehiel, a descendant of Gershon.

The people rejoiced over the offerings, for they had given freely and wholeheartedly to the Lord, and King David was filled with joy.

I am also reminded that Jesus led a Tax Specialist called Zacchaeus and his house to salvation (Luke 19: 1 - 10). What we know is that being a tax specialist was not, and till now, is not a sin but a job or function. Tax collection was Zacchaeus's job. He must have been gifted in mathematical computations and tax efficiency. It was his abuse of his talent that resulted in him becoming a thief. While taxing people, Zacchaeus took extra for himself. I think that he still had his talent when he was saved. After being saved, with an instantly renewed mind and transformation sipping in, Zacchaeus said, "Behold Lord, half of my goods I give to the poor. And if I have defrauded anyone of anything, I restore it fourfold." We gain useful insight; he was not just giving away half his assets; he was returning four times as much to every individual he had cheated. Only shrewd investors are capable of as high as 400% return. Considering that Zacchaeus was giving half of his possessions, giving away such returns was phenomenal. We need people with renewed minds and skills like those of Zacchaeus, people who are passionate about others, those who realise and understand that they are blessed to be a blessing.

It is clear that Zacchaeus had a family. Jesus said, "Today salvation has come to this house…" And because of this, he too would have transferred wealth and passed on skills to another generation. Anyone learning from him should have taken the tax specialist and tax collection profession to the next level (excluding defrauding other people).

Now picture yourself a son and an heir in Solomon's position. The road has been made clearer, provision is bountiful, you have a conditionally guaranteed future, the map is set before you, and the strategy is faultless. How can you fail? Why would you consider alternatives? Is it possible that you can be distracted? Things are done for you, not as a show for the world to see. It is not for you to owe gratitude to your parents, but for you to see the awesomeness of Almighty God, as well as to acknowledge God's provision, dwell where He is, and dare to walk with Him in unchartered territory.

True sons discern the leading of God, recognise and respect God's delegated authority over their lives, run with the vision heralded, are obedient, receive the mantle or baton, and run to accomplish and impact others. It is important for finances to come into the Body of Christ. As long as money is in the wrong hands, the problems seen and experienced will not be solved. Wealthy people must also be found in the Church, people who understand the real value and meaning of money. Just as David provided for Solomon, let us make provision and equip the future generations, so that the world can be envious, curious, amazed, inquisitive, and come to know Jesus Christ.

Each generation has a responsibility to pass on or hand over something. Not everyone is cash or asset rich. However, you do have something; for example, your wealth creation plans and ideas are your baton. Do not let those ideas die unheard and unspoken; refuse to let them be buried with you. It has been said that the richest place on earth is a graveyard—here lie people, who died with great ideas and potential, but who did not have the stomach, or initiative, to exercise that potential and step out. It is better to be God's failure, having tried, than to die with 'dignity', having not even challenged a mouse to a battle.

GENERATIONAL TRANSFORMERS

Psalms 32: 8

The Lord says, "I will guide you along the best pathway for your life. I will advise you and watch over you."

I Peter 5: 1 – 3

*And now, a word to you who are elders in the churches. I, too, am an elder and a witness to the sufferings of Christ. And I, too, will share his glory and his honour when he returns. As a fellow elder, this is my appeal to you: Care for the flock of God **entrusted** to you. Watch over it willingly, not grudgingly—not for what you will get out of it, but because you are eager to serve God. Don't lord it over the people assigned to your care but **lead them by your good example**.*

I Corinthians 4: 15 -16 (The Message)

I'm not writing all this as a neighbourhood scold just to make you feel rotten. I'm writing as a father to you, my children. I love you and want you to grow up well, not spoiled. There are a lot of people around who can't wait to tell you what you've done wrong, but there aren't many fathers willing to take the time and effort to help you grow up. It was as Jesus helped me proclaim God's message to you that I became your father. I'm not, you know, asking you to do anything I'm not already doing myself.

Psalm 100: 5 is a verse packed with continuity and inheritance. It also reminds us that God is good, His mercy is everlasting and that His truth endures to *all* generations. God is love and is merciful, and His plan has always been about forever. He is not just interested in one generation but *all* generations.

Proverbs 22: 6 reminds us that we should train or start children off on the way they should go, and even when they are old, they will not turn from it. This scripture covers so much, including their walk with God, how they carry themselves before man and even their character. James Moffatt translates another aspect of this verse that I want to layout in this book. James Moffatt says, 'Train a child for his *proper trade*, and he will never leave it when he is old.' The picture painted here is that the 'parent' must assist children to identify what they are supposed to do here on earth. Proper trade speaks of God's purpose or the reason you exist. So, whether you are a parent, a pastor, a teacher, a student, a mentor, a mentee, or prophet—make sure that you are in your proper trade. Make sure that you are in your lane; don't run another person's race or cut in on anyone—even when others are drawn to the latest craze, stay the course. Keep on the lookout for my other book, *"Sweet spot -living in His presence,"* where I deal with this matter is greater detail.

When we embrace and walk into our purpose, God will guide you along the best pathway for your life, He will advise you and watch over you. We will encounter many people in our path, who we must make every effort to see grow in relationship with God. Our lives must be full of Christ, and God will then entrust them to us. Parents guard their heart and soul, lest they forget the things their eyes have seen, and make them known to their children, and their children's children [Deuteronomy 4: 9]. They are God-fearing, keep His commands and instil the same to their descendants [Deuteronomy 5: 29]. Their primary purpose, as all of us, must be to please God. It is not an accident or pure coincident that Jesus, said, 'Seek first the Kingdom of God and His righteousness and all these things shall be added to you' [Matthew 6: 33].

As we lead in the primary, they will follow each of us as we follow Christ. The additional responsibility here is to assist them identify their function in God's kingdom. Romans 12: 4 - 5 says, 'Just as our bodies have many parts and each part has a special function, so it is with Christ's Body. We are all parts of His Body, and each of us has different work to do.' Children are supposed to live in their sweet spot, living out God's dreams and not walking another man's path. For example, some will be in the five-fold ministry [Ephesians 4: 11]; others will be doctors, lawyers, administrators, politicians, gardeners, nurses, technocrats, worship leaders or chefs. It is recognising that God has given these different gifts for doing all these certain things. When you live in your sweet spot, you will encourage others to do the same, influencing them to pursue excellence, to no longer remain stagnant, and to refuse to be one dimensional, but constantly pursue improvement and natural progression. These people will graduate their steps of obedience, and will hear the voice of the Lord saying, 'This is the way, walk ye in it, when ye turn to the right hand, and when ye turn to the left' [Isaiah 30: 21 KJV].

In the Old Testament, the priests, prophets, and kings were anointed with oil for service. We too must nominate, designate, or choose strategically and by divine election, those following our example as successors or leading candidates for an office, for a function, and for being and doing. With wisdom, we need to confer by divine prompting, consecrate, anoint, invest, induct, appoint, install, and bless the coming generations. We must not just appoint for the sake of fulfilling a role.

I have been in church circles for some time and have observed some uncomfortable, cringe-worthy and stomach curling things. Some men and women [parents, mentors] have irresponsibly thrust youth into ego feeding environments, as well as handing over everything—assets, businesses and ministries—to their 'sons' based solely on hereditary grounds, having the right "name." Oftentimes, these 'youth' have not had the character, the calling, the spiritual or natural gift, and the capacity [spiritual, emotional, mental, and physical]. Appointing has been based on preference rather than conviction, perception and not reality and appearance rather than authenticity. These parents and mentors have often missed and overlooked God's best. As a result, these spoilt 'kids' squander their inheritance. Some of the appointed have turned previously anointed praise and worship times, where God is the centre, into well-organised popular concerts glorifying the flesh. They have run church ministries into monuments, and some have run businesses into liquidation.

Ultimately, the Kingdom suffers, and continuity ceases. There is nothing wrong with giving paternal children and mentees things. There is a problem when it is clear that they have no desire to fulfil God's mission. They will destroy that which God has begun. Let each youth and mentee be like David, [I Samuel 17: 32 - 40]. Refuse the mantle that is not yours; it might be too heavy, too big, and very awkward to wear. Know your identity and do not be intimidated, even when all you carry is unorthodox—a sling and a bag of stones. Every day, each of us is directly and indirectly influencing people around us. Let us be more aware of those that can move God's Kingdom forward. If we look and apply things according to the flesh, ultimately the kingdom will suffer, and God will have to start all over again.

I Peter 5: 1 - 3 and I Corinthians 4: 15 -16 are Heaven's expectation of what responsible mothers, fathers and mentors look like. They never push those that follow onto roads they have never walked. In addition, in Titus 2: 2 - 5 in his letter to Titus, Paul urges Titus to teach correct healthy living. Upon closer observations, you will see that continuity is at the very core of his letter; It all began with Jesus, then onto Paul is being handed to Titus, who in turn is to stir the older men [and women, as well as those who are spiritually mature], to impart to the coming generations.

'Teach the older men to exercise self-control, to be worthy of respect, and to live wisely. They must have strong faith and be filled with love and patience. Similarly, teach the older women to live in a way that is appropriate for someone serving the Lord. They must not go around speaking evil of others and must not be heavy drinkers. Instead, they should teach others what is good. These older women must train the younger women to love their husbands and their children, to live wisely and be pure, to take care of their homes, to do good, and to be submissive to their husbands. Then they will not bring shame on the word of God.'

This truth will ensure that when Jesus returns, He will certainly find authentic followers of the Way.

We all need sons [those who have the early Church DNA]. If the truth be told, each of us long to have an heir, a successor, or someone who we can influence and propel into the future, someone who will continue what we initiate. We need responsible people who will carry the Name of Jesus, the vision He commissioned us, and our values. They will inherit and take something from us into tomorrow, one who will continue the legacy, one who will slay giants and will expand the kingdom. Our passion and drive for sons and daughters of the faith must not be for selfish reasons. It must be to introduce them to our loving Father and bring them into more.

See what the father of faith did. Abraham believed God and did not think of himself as too old. The Lord spoke to Abram in a vision and said to him, "Do not be afraid, Abram, for I will protect you, and your reward will be great." But Abram replied, "O Sovereign Lord, what good are all your blessings when I don't even have a son? Since I don't have a son, Eliezer of Damascus, a servant in my household, will inherit all my wealth. You have given me no children, so one of my servants will have to be my heir." Then the Lord said to him, "No, your servant will not be your heir, for you will have a son of your own to inherit everything I am giving you." Then the Lord brought Abram outside beneath the night sky and told him, "Look up into the heavens and count the stars if you can. Your descendants will be like that—too many to count!" And Abram believed the Lord, and the Lord declared him righteous because of his faith.

In Luke 7: 11 - 17, Jesus was moved with compassion when He encountered a widow whose only son had died. He knew that this was a dire situation. It was probably the end of the family line and possibly the end of her source of income and livelihood. Her son's death would have likely been the end of her life. She would have been slowly sapped out of joy and may have ended up being on her deathbed. The love of God stretched out, touched the corpse, and just as He [God, the Father] that spoke the earth into existence, He [Jesus] called the son back from the dead. The son sat up and began to speak.

All predecessors need to hand over the baton. The Bible says that God [the Father] so loved the world that He gave us Jesus, so that we become Christ-like [John 3: 16]. Giving is taking what one owns or possesses and passing it on. The giver often hopes and desires that the recipient will treat that which he or she has been given, with due care, responsibility, and aspirations of going further. One of the first things Man was endowed with was to possess and have dominion over creatures on earth. This is a picture of God saying to Man, "As I am to all spiritual and physical, I give you dominance in every sphere of life." He also told Man to multiply—continuity! Isn't it amazing how we can learn from nature? Nature procreates, and we get a vast array of colours, and creatures—that is continuity. We need to have the same joy when we hand over, transfer, or pass on what we possess. In Luke 12: 32, it says that it is the Father's good pleasure to give us the kingdom— that's God's rule and reign in and through us.

Abram's faith impressed God so much [Hebrews 11: 9] that God was moved and changed Abram's name to Abraham, a father of many nations [Genesis 17: 5]. God promised to make Abraham exceedingly fruitful, and birth nations from him. Today, we stand as his seed. In 1 Corinthians 4: 15 – 16, Paul made an observation that there are many teachers in the Church but very few fathers. Paul must have been prompted by the Holy Spirit to write this. All through Paul's letters, he distinguishes his personal opinions and often distinguishes them from that which is from God. In this instance, we can safely say that God revealed this to Paul. The truth is that we all have the potential to teach and correct each other about various things; however, fathering is altogether different. Simply because you are a sperm donor or ovary carrier, have the potential to procreate and provide physical needs— food, water, clothing, and shelter for your children—does not make you a father or responsible parent. You are not a spiritual mother just because you dress smart, receive compliments, turn heads as you walk past, speak eloquently, and say the right things in public.

A father or mother is one who has a child [seed]. Fathers are seed carriers, producers, authors, and generators or founders of a line or family. Mothers incubate, nurture, and monitor growth in a place of love and tender care. Just like Moses, each of us must grow from knowing God's acts to knowing His ways [Psalm 103: 7, Isaiah 55: 9]. Like in the parable of the Sower [Luke 8: 1 -5, Matthew 13: 1 23 & Mark 4: 1 - 20], we are to scatter the seed into good ground in order to reproduce in abundance. If the seed remains stored in a bag, it will not improve in quality or quantity; it will not change in size, number, or weight. In fact, the seed can ultimately rot and become useless. As we align our ways with God, He will watch over everything we do in line with His will to ensure continuity; vitality, soundness, and strength [Isaiah 55: 10 - 11]. The reminder to each father, mother, and mentor is that, unless the seed falls to the ground and dies, it remains only a single seed, but if it dies, it bears much fruit [John 12: 24 paraphrased]. Any parent caught up in self, ego, selfish ambition and failure to impart that which God has instructed, can cause everything to dry up and cease when they die.

Parents are the source and originator of something. They accept and acknowledge responsibility and do not shy away. They bring love, care, identity, belongingness, are providers and protectors. Fathers are active, are interested and get involved in the welfare and wellbeing of their children. Good parents are regularly available and meet emotional needs, providing affirmation and approval. They are warm, extend forgiveness, and are constantly looking out for prodigals. They wield power and influence, bringing strength and stability. Good fathers offer guidance and protection; they are relentless in their quest to provide for their children. Fathers impart vision and direction; they are trusted counsellors or guides, instil discipline, and they are a model character and they birth longevity in their children. Good parents want their children to go further and attain greater things than themselves.

For 400 years, when Man had withdrawn from God, preceding the arrival of John the Baptist, Zechariah his father and Elizabeth his mother [Luke 1: 5 - 25] had a holy discontent and dissatisfaction at the status quo. They were pioneers in reengaging with God; their zeal and passion were relayed to their seed, John who became the greatest prophet of the Old Testament. We don't commend his parents enough, but Zechariah and Elizabeth were excellent parents. Further to my explanation about sons being arrows [see Chapter: Aggregation of Experiences], I want to build on it and show what good fathers in God's House look like.

II Kings 13:14-19

Now when Elisha had fallen sick with the illness of which he was to die, Joash king of Israel went down to him and wept before him, crying, "My father, my father! The chariots of Israel and its horsemen!" And Elisha said to him, "Take a bow and arrows." So, he took a bow and arrows. Then he said to the king of Israel, "Draw the bow," and he drew it. And Elisha laid his hands on the king's hands. And he said, "Open the window eastward," and he opened it. Then Elisha said, "Shoot," and he shot. And he said, "The LORD's arrow of victory, the arrow of victory over Syria! For you shall fight the Syrians in Aphek until you have made an end of them." And he said, "Take the arrows," and he took them. And he said to the king of Israel, "Strike the ground with them." And he struck three times and stopped. Then the man of God was angry with him and said, "You should have struck five or six times; then you would have struck down Syria until you had made an end of it, but now you will strike down Syria only three times."

Joash had heard the legacy of Elisha's cry when Elijah was taken by the chariots of fire [II Kings 2: 12]. What Joash did not realise is that words were not enough [let this be a lesson, even to young men in our day]. Just because you dress and talk like your father or leaders, it does not mean that you carry the same anointing; you must first and foremost develop your character and then desire the mantle. Joash's understanding was historic, and he did not have the revelation of a required deeper walk with God and a higher path to elevate into. He wanted the bells and whistles but did not know how to truly earn the stripes. He was able to shoot the arrows, which was easy, but when it came to strike the ground, the vibrations moved into his arms and body; it was painful, and he tired after three strikes. We need to go beyond the pain and self-dignity thresholds and have the spiritual and physical fortitude to go on and keep on going.

Our sons [arrows] must strike a killer blow to doubt, fear, compromise, passivity, unbelief, timidity, and the lack of continuity. They need to impose and rubber-stamp themselves that they have arrived, from the rising of the sun right through to its setting. Fathers in each generation must aggressively strike the ground not once or three times but strike it countless times and never stop. Strategically, this must be for the health and well-being of sons. Affliction shall not arise the second time; bad habits will not raise their ugly heads in the Church. She shall be radiant, beaming with light, well flavoured with saltiness as She matures in power, stature, and influence. There is nothing that this world has to offer that can cause Her to take Her eyes off Her Beloved. Until the arrival of her Groom, the Body of Christ will occupy and stand strong.

Fathers are those who are: Lovers of God, are a demonstration of God in Man, are God's mouthpiece, command respect, are bold, are sources of encouragement, are disciplinarians, good examples, and models, and are a place of refuge.

It is interesting, when we look at Paul's statement in his letter to the Church at Corinth, that he says that 'in Christ Jesus,' he became a father to them. We know that he was not their biological father; Paul never married and had no paternal children, read I Corinthians 7. His sole commitment was to please God. The Church at Corinth became his adopted children. Paul, therefore, shows that being a father is not solely governed by paternity. Paul became a spiritual father. Later in the same letter, Paul also refers to Timothy as his son.

I Corinthians 4: 17 (NIV)
For this reason, I have sent to you Timothy, my son whom I love, who is faithful in the Lord. He will remind you of my way of life in Christ Jesus, which agrees with what I teach everywhere in every church.

Paul not only just calls Timothy his son, but he also emphasises that he loves him—that is affirmation or the wind in a sail that can take a son to the finish line. Also, notice this, after Jesus was baptised by John, God the Father said:

This is my beloved Son, in whom I am well pleased.

Timothy, like his spiritual father Paul, also went to preach and teach the Word of God everywhere, and in Christ Jesus, Timothy went on to father others. Novices need to be trained in the trades and areas we see and know that God is directing them, so that they become sufficiently skilled, responsible, and mature enough to handle the things of God. God has anointed and called some people to what is termed secular employment to govern, to network, to be leading industrialists and some to become economists.

The story of Abraham and Lot has so much we can and should learn. One aspect from the story I would like to highlight is the father heart of Abraham. He loved Lot and wanted the best for him. He asked Lot to choose the land he wanted to settle in, and after Lot had done so, Abraham settled in what would have looked like the less fertile land. He placed Lot above himself. He was truly humble. He treated Lot as a son. I must however also add this; we need to be fathers and mentors with discernment. Let us rightly distinguish what God is calling each of us specifically [and not have appendages or parasites that take the life out of us]. We need to be careful not to promote our children or those we mentor and watch over into trades or ministries to fulfil our own selfish desires or dreams, as well as to cover up our own failings from our youth. Let us be so sensitive, have integrity, honour God and be his mouth and hands, guiding God's people into their God given destiny. We need to hold this responsibility with fear and trembling as one day we will all stand before Him and give an account for these "little" ones.

The Church more than ever needs to emphasise with a loud voice that calling and destiny is not just in the fivefold ministry, Ephesians 4: 11. We have not audibly encouraged people who are called to the marketplace, to be sculptors, painters, businessmen, economists, doctors, engineers, pilots, accountants, and leaders of countries, to go—not to pervert, idolise, or be identified by the gift. We were all born with gifts that God has endowed. We did not have to work hard to earn them. They are God given, and our part is to receive and then exercise those gifts. If we are to encourage the coming generations to live and not just exist, we need to help them to function, in their gifts, which are their sweet spots. We must supplement this with our experience, getting them to study and encouraging them in order to make them more rounded and stronger.

Lately especially in the marketplace, I have observed two trains of thought: Firstly, let a person just operate from their gift, and the other thought overly emphasises acquiring a good education as the solution to life. I believe the answer is somewhere in the middle as there is no single solution that fits all. Let us help identify the gifts and calling of God, and let us train the generations, encourage competency through obtaining qualifications and then let us release them, so that they see God working in and through them in greater measure.

Let us live in harmony with each other. Let each of our very lives complement each other. Let us not think we know it all and also not try and act important [by intimidating, manipulation or controlling others], but let us enjoy the company of ordinary people.

The Bible says:

Romans 11: 29
For the gifts and calling of God are irrevocable.

Proverbs 22: 6 *(Moffatt Translation)*
*Train a child for his **proper trade**, and he will never leave it when he is old.*

Proverbs 18: 16
A man's gift makes room for him and brings him before great men.

The people God called impacted and totally transformed were not lazy or idle. These were generally skilled or competent in their trades; Peter, Andrew, James, and John were fishermen [Matthew 4: 18 - 22], Matthew was a tax collector and accountant [Matthew 9: 9], Simon the zealot had political affiliations, Zacchaeus was a tax collector [Luke 19: 1 - 10], Dorcas manufactured and designed clothes [Acts 9: 39], and Paul was a tentmaker by trade [Acts 18: 3]. The list is endless.

David must have been thrilled at seeing with his own eyes, the manifestation of a promise, Solomon becoming king [I Kings 1: 48]. Notice how David was a warrior, and yet he was sensible enough not to expect any of his sons to be like him. Sons do not have to go into the ministry [unless called by God] or duplicate their fathers because they are pastors. Similarly, they do not become businesspeople because of a long line or heritage of trade people in the family. Wise men and women of God, good fathers, father figures, parents, spiritual parents, and mentors discern the leading of God, nurture and encourage sons into their destiny. The common link is that they love God, walk with God, and find their identity rooted in God.

David also acknowledged Solomon's 'youth' and inexperience to the people [I Chronicles 29: 1]. There was a daunting task ahead of Solomon, which he could have chosen to do alone and his way, but David reminded Solomon to choose God first.

I Chronicles 28: 9 *(AMP)*
And you, Solomon, my son, know the God of your father [have personal knowledge of Him, be acquainted with, and understand Him; appreciate, heed, and cherish Him] and serve Him with a blameless

heart and a willing mind. For the Lord searches all hearts and minds and understands all the wanderings of the thoughts. If you seek Him [inquiring for and of Him and requiring Him as your first and vital necessity], you will find Him; but if you forsake Him, He will cast you off forever!

God handpicked Solomon amongst his brothers. He was not chosen because he looked more handsome and not because he was eloquent or had better negotiating skills [I Chronicles 28: 5 - 6]. He was selected to build the house of God and to lead the nation of Israel and all David, his father, did was to comply with God. As a son, it did not mean that Solomon was more unique than his brothers. When others are being singled out, receiving prophecy, and encouragement, we need to remain fresh in the Word, full of the Holy Spirit and remember that we are each still the apple of His eye. He allowed His only begotten Son to come to earth. Jesus took up frail humanity, was crucified, died, and rose again, and He did it all for you. When you know what you are supposed to be doing, you will not be embarrassed or intimidated by anyone. You will grow in confidence in Him and begin to realise that in God, you are complete, lacking nothing.

We need good fathers, the same as Uri and Ahisamach in the Old Testament; parents who care and are not just teachers, instructors and guides. Let us be those who refuse to be ordinary, reject being carbon copies of previously failed generations. We need to go down in the history books as having left a legacy for others. Let us help others enter their promise land. Let us assist others in finding their special assignment, discovering their mission inspire them to identify their sweet spot, to minister out of the overflow and encourage them to walk in their God-given destiny. We need to inspire and ignite vision. Vision is the reason why things come into existence and manifestation. For example with Joseph [Genesis], despite all the hardships, it was the vision and purpose of God that made him complete his race. Notice what God said to Moses,

[Exodus 31: 2 - 6]. Concerning Bezaleel and Aholiab, these two were set apart to be amongst fellow professionals. They were unique, and they excelled and were the best at what they did.

Exodus 31: 2 - 6 (KJV)
See, I have called by name Bezaleel the son of Uri, the son of Hur, of the tribe of Judah: And I have filled him with the spirit of God, in wisdom, and in knowledge, and in all manner of workmanship, to devise cunning works, to work in gold, and in silver, and in brass, and in cutting of stones, to set them, and in carving of timber, to work in all manner of workmanship. And I, behold, I have given with him Aholiab, the son of Ahisamach, of the tribe of Dan: and in the hearts of all that are wise-hearted, I have put wisdom, that they may make all that I have commanded thee.

These two men amongst other skilled artisans were singled out by God. They had skills, wisdom, and ability in their trades. Did these skills suddenly fall upon them from the sky? In my imagination, these two, from an early age, would have had a burning desire to become skilled artisans. Their parents would have noticed the gifts and their willingness to excel. Their parents probably taught them or found the appropriate teachers. They encouraged their sons to pursue their God-given dream and may have even introduced them to the more experienced tradesman to hone their skills—that is true stewardship. Bezaleel and Aholiab were anointed and called into their trades, and they excelled beyond their parents' and mentors' levels and others' expectations.

In my imagination, I believe that Uri, the father of Bezaleel and Ahisamach, the father of Aholiab, did not irritate or impose their thinking upon their sons. I believe that these two parents saw what God was doing, and years later, they saw the manifestation or fruit when the boys became men.

The Bible says:

Ephesians 6: 4 (AMP)
Fathers, do not irritate and provoke your children to anger [do not exasperate them to resentment], but rear them [tenderly] in the training and discipline and the counsel and admonition of the Lord.

In contrast, can you imagine yourself being Kish, the father of Saul [I Samuel 9], or Jesse, the father of David [I Samuel 17]? Did these two parents know that they were living with the next great move of God in Israel? Did they have discernment? Were they in tune with God? Their sons would turn out to be history makers, shake nations, and transform generations. Put crudely; it seems Kish and Jesse's individual roles were accomplished at conception. Both men were men of power, influence, and wealth and had some form of recognition in their environment. We have no reason to believe nor are we given any indication of any interest or positive influence they had in their two sons' lives. These two fathers clearly lacked something and failed in their responsibility to steward God's boys.

The Bible is explicit; Saul was herding donkeys, and in his time, David was shepherding sheep. Both Saul and David were tasked by their fathers to be out with the animals. It gives us some useful insight into these two fathers. Jesse probably thought David looked like a sheep, smelled like a sheep, and acted like a sheep. In fact, when the prophet came to anoint God's chosen, Jesse had forgotten to summon David to the meeting. On the other hand, Kish made Saul look for donkeys even though he had servants who could have accomplished the task. Furthermore, Kish instructed Saul to go with the servants on the search for the donkeys. It appears to me; Kish did not see the difference between his son and his servant.

In the absence of earthly fathers, God groomed both boys [Saul and David] Himself, and they eventually became men of power. Saul and David grew, not because of what they saw, being modelled by their fathers. In the wilderness alone looking after the donkeys and sheep,

God gave these boys lessons. Saul and David had hunger, desire, and passion; the kind which attracted God on the scene. There in the wild, with none to impress, God Himself nurtured, refined, and turned them into real men. Saul and David were rough diamonds; they were not flawless. I believe their limitations and frailty as men were because of the lack of human input [absent fathers]. Who would they have learned and seen Godly character from?

Fathers can shape character. They induce faith by being adverts as they demonstrate how things are to be done. They continually challenge sons to ensure competency is attained. They stand in the grandstands applauding and encouraging, watching over and witnessing new levels of excellence being attained. Fathers must also be the initiators of succession planning, ensuring that someone takes over and continues the race. They do not manipulate or intimidate children and those who they watch over or have a delegated responsibility over. They do not detour them from their race and destination that God has set for them. Instead, they remind themselves that people are children of God. Each of us is supposed to have the attitude of Hannah who said, give me a son; I will give him to the Lord all his life [I Samuel 1: 11].

There are few good fathers, both in the Church and in the world. Just as it was in the days of Noah, so it is in our time. Shockingly, cohabiting has become socially acceptable and normal, even amongst born-again believers. Everything is being done based on convenience; a man can live with a woman and have children with her without commitment. Instead of married couples, we have settled for partnerships, and instead of fathers in the house, we now have libertines. It sounds extreme, but this is the reality. Fewer men are ready to embrace responsibility. There is a cry for fathers to stand up and shape the moral fabric of our society, built on the Word of God.

In the Bible, we see how parents encouraged the next generation.

- Moses to Joshua: Have I not commanded you? **Be strong, vigorous, and very courageous**. Be not afraid, neither be dismayed, for the Lord your God is with you wherever you go [Joshua 1:9].

- David to Solomon: **Be strong and courageous** and do it. Fear not, be not dismayed, for the Lord God, my God, is with you. He will not fail or forsake you until you have finished all the work for the service of the house of the Lord [I Chronicles 28:20].
- Paul to Timothy: So, you, my son, **be strong**, strengthened inwardly in the grace that is found only in Christ Jesus [II Timothy 2:1].

What instructions are we passing onto the next fathers, mothers, leaders, apostles, prophets, and businesspeople? Spiritual fathers are qualified by experience. These are men of God, who walk with and know God intimately. They, with godly wisdom, will counsel and point sons into new heights and depths in God, so that children finish their race stronger.

Deuteronomy 11:19 - 21 (KJV)
And ye shall teach them your children, speaking of them when thou sittest in thine house, and when thou walkest by the way, when thou liest down, and when thou risest up. And thou shalt write them upon the door posts of thine house, and upon thy gates: That your days may be multiplied, and the days of your children, in the land which the Lord sware unto your fathers to give them, as the days of heaven upon the earth.

To those women reading this book who think I am just concentrating on the impact that Men have done, please continue to read. Just as Abraham was to Isaac [Genesis], Jedidah [a woman] was to Josiah [II Kings 22], Hannah [another woman] was to Samuel [I Samuel], David was to Solomon [Kings & Chronicles], Elizabeth [another woman] was to John the Baptist [Luke 1: 41], Mary [another woman] was to Jesus [Matthew, Mark, Luke, & John], Eunice [yet another woman] was to Timothy [I Timothy 1: 5] and Paul was to Timothy, the Church and generations are desperate for authentic spiritual parents. The Bible shows us how God uses imperfect vessels to impact and father generations. Have you ever written yourself off because you have natural limitations? For example, Noah was a drunk, Jacob was a thief, Moses was of limited speech and likely stammered, Peter was impetuous, and Paul was a murderer. You and I would have probably written these people off, but God didn't. All of these men transformed generations!

CHILDREN OF THE HOUSE OF GOD

II Timothy 3: 14 - 15
*But as for you, continue in what you have learned and have become convinced of, because you know those from whom you learned it, and how from **infancy** you have known the Holy Scriptures, which are able to make you wise for salvation through faith in Christ Jesus.*

Ephesians 5: 1 (AMP)
Therefore, become imitators of God [copy Him and follow His example], as well-beloved children [imitate their father].

Proverbs 22: 6 (NIV)
*Start children off on the way **they should go**, and even when they are old, they will not turn from it.*

Wise children make their fathers proud of them; foolish ones bring their mothers grief [Proverbs 10: 1]. Let us therefore make our parents, father figures and spiritual parents beam with pride. Let them not hold their heads down with shame or cause them to have sleepless nights because of our ways. Children in the House of God, first and foremost are secure and know their identity in Christ. They do not allow anyone to look down on them because they are young, they are examples to all believers, in word, in conversation, in love, in spirit, in faith and in purity [I Timothy 4: 12]. They are faith-filled and Spirit filled, they dream dreams, see visions, and prophesy [Joel 2: 28] In the presence of authentic children of God, there is conviction. The hearts of parents turn back to God, aged men become sober, grave, temperate, sound in faith, in love and in patience. The aged women's behaviour become flavoured with holiness and adorned with good things.

Understand this; there is no Samuel the prophet without Eli. The Bible reminds us that when we were children, we talked, thought, and reasoned like children, but as we matured, we put childish things away [I Corinthians 13: 11]. When you were born again, your inner man or spirit was a spiritual baby [I Peter 2: 2]. But thank God for the Holy Ghost and Word, we grow up into spiritual Manhood [Hebrews 5: 12 – 14]. In I Samuel 3, a youthful Samuel could not distinguish God's voice. Three times the Lord called Samuel and he mistook it to be Eli summoning him. It was eventually, Eli's discernment, his experience and instruction to Samuel, that transitioned Samuel from a child to sonship, from a spiritual babe to a spiritual man, and from a naturally ordinary person to a supernaturally ordinary vessel and prophet of God. Sons and daughters in the House desire nothing except dancing to an audience of One, our Heavenly Father—who we were introduced to by our Lord and Saviour Jesus Christ, through our pastors, parents, friends, mentors, teachers or evangelists.

In II Chronicles 26, the Bible highlights mentorship of Uzziah by Zechariah. Uzziah became king of Judah aged sixteen and reigned in Jerusalem for fifty-two years. This puts perspective on time. What you and I may think is a long time can be temporary in the eyes of God. Verse 5 says that while Zechariah mentored Uzziah, the king sought God, and the Lord gave him success. We are mentored, so that we embrace what we have been taught, and that at some stage we graduate our steps to militarily walk in the Holy Spirit, and then, we too one day become mentors. Uzziah did not do so; he died a miserable, sad death.

The drive by parents, mentors, or teachers to initiate, to teach, to share, to transfer, to impart and pass the mantle should be simulated by pursuing sons with a complete yieldedness to God; humility, willing hearts, a holy restlessness, and a determination to go further, for absolute continuity to be birthed. Just like in a relay race, all sons need to learn to humbly receive the baton. Sons are not servants, who just follow their master's orders [sometimes blindly or ignorantly]. We also know that servants, in turn expect a financial reward—not necessarily the case with sons. Sons are not hirelings, who are paid for doing a job that is not respected or that is considered morally wrong. Sons and daughters are not only biological but spiritual. They are a sum total of their parents [Hebrews 1: 3 and John 14: 9], are exact replicas of their parent, are seed carriers, are heirs, and need to be nurtured to grow. Spiritual sons or spiritual children must first recognise, understand, and know their spiritual fathers and mentors. True spiritual fathers and mentors carry your next level. They understand where you are going and will catapult you into your destiny.

Here is the instruction we should give sons in God's house; "If you obey the commandments of the Lord your God that I command you today, by loving the Lord your God, by walking in His ways, and by keeping His commandments and His statutes and His rules, then you shall live and multiply, and the Lord your God will bless you in the land that you are entering to take possession of it." [Deuteronomy 30: 16 & Isaiah 1: 19].

Furthermore, children in the House also need to honour their earthly parents:

Ephesians 6:2 (AMP)
Honour (esteem and value as precious) your father and your mother— this is the first commandment with a promise.

God gives a reward to each of us who honour our parents, our spiritual parents, father figures, pastors, and mentors. This will directly impact our potential to influence others and the coming generations—long life means greater potential to impact.

A son honours his father and a servant his master, just the same way we honour God, our Heavenly Father. 'Then if I am a Father, where is My honour? And if I am a Master, where is my respect?' [Malachi 1: 6a]. As the Father gave [John 3: 16 & Luke 12: 32], let us honour and respect Him. A son must honour his earthly father, mother, or mentor.

Let me shed a bit of light; the story of the prodigal son [Luke 15: 11 - 32] is a very deep story. I want to focus on the son's question to his father.

He was actually quite bold. He was unsatisfied with where he was, desired more and decided to do something about it. He approached his father and said, "Give me my inheritance." Ultimately, discussions must be amicable, and one must move on well. Now imagine having the right motive, and having the same boldness, as you approach our Heavenly Father. True sons need to have a holy boldness, a discontent of the status-quo, and must be looking forward. Our demand must be from a pure heart. Caleb's expression "give me this mountain!" [Joshua 6: 12] is a good example. Maturity is not borne from age alone, but also from experience. Caleb's picture of inheritance was not just centred on self. The Bible says that Hebron still belongs to the descendants of Caleb, the son of Jephunneh the Kenizzite, because he faithfully obeyed the Lord, the God of Israel. Our attitude must always be Christ-like. Remember Jesus at the well with the Samaritan woman [John 4: 7], He asked, "Give me a drink." The outcome of Jesus' thirst for water resulted in giving life, as the news about the kingdom spread—that is continuity! What have you been asking for? What is your thirst? What has been its outcome?

A life that follows or imitates Christ looks something like this [John 12: 49 and Proverbs 4: 20]: As a son, you speak those things that your Father has taught. You stick to the assignment alone. Secondly, John 5: 19 a son will only do the things the Father has instructed. When we look at Christ's example, it blows everything else out of the park. In John 17: 20 – 26, Jesus is praying for us. He also confirms that He and the Father are in us. This is the mystery of the Gospel. The very life of God is in us, and we are to carry out His purposes and plans, precept upon precept here on earth. God's plans are eternal; therefore, our lives must align to Him accordingly.

Jesus said that we should abide in Him and His Word in us, for without Him we cannot do anything [John 15: 4 - 7]. The Bible says sons of God are led by His Holy Spirit [Romans 8: 14]. To be led means our whole being in total wilful surrender, obedience, and complete alignment with the mind, the will, the intention, and the purposes of God. It is where the person of the Holy Spirit is in complete control, and where we live unreservedly for and through Him. Life in the Holy Spirit is not about picking our moments when it suits us, meandering between the flesh and Spirit, being carnal and spiritual. It is about crucifying the flesh, dying daily, and bringing the flesh into subjection. As sons we need to know what God says and requires of us, as well as obey our earthly parents, mentors and God's delegated authority [Church leadership].

As a son and true example of how a child in the House of God should be, Jesus evidently understood the plan of the Father. He took heed of the instructions He had received before leaving His throne and coming down to earth. As a son, can you take instructions? Will you finish stronger than those who have gone before you? Everything that Jesus did was very God in His actions and deeds. See this:

John 5:19-20 (ESV)
So, Jesus said to them, "Truly, truly, I say to you, the Son can do nothing of his own accord, but only what he sees the Father doing. For whatever the Father does, that the Son does likewise. For the Father loves the Son and shows him all that he himself is doing. And greater works than these will he show him so that you may marvel.

In addition, everything that Jesus said was from the Father [John 12: 49]. It no longer surprises me why the Bible encourages us to be swift to listen, slow to speak, and slow to anger [James 1: 19]. We are reminded that the tongue is a fire [James 3: 6 - 8]. We need to bridle the tongue. With it, we bless God and yet curse fellow Man. Death and life lie in the power of the tongue [Proverbs 6: 2 & 18: 21]. We therefore need to be consistent and stable in all our speech both privately and publicly, for a double-minded person is unstable [James 1: 8]; unstable means prone to change, unsteady, wobbly, to give way, and volatile.

Another thing is that children need to identify and understand what their God given trade and task is. Once identified and understood, apply yourself and accomplish the task! Jesus did, and He accomplished the Father's task [the business] that the Father set for Him. The Son recognised His business and walked in it. Jesus confirmed this when He said this:

John 17: 4 & 5 *(KJV)*
*I have glorified thee on earth by **accomplishing the work that thou gavest me to do**; now Father glorify me in thy presence with the glory which I enjoyed in thy presence before the world began.*

When people are saved, mentorship must be encouraged and prioritised – I don't mean systems and programs. If the Church misunderstands or does not mentor, what are the chances that anyone will ever understand fathering the coming generations? God saves us as children; He expects us to mature that we too finish the race as parents, impacting generations. David was a man of God, a psalmist, a warrior, a husband, father, King, prophet, and priest—but ultimately, a son of God. In my view, when God looked at his son David, He [God] loved him so much that He [God] said, "If I take up the form of a Man, I want to be called your son." Generations later, when you look at the genealogy of Jesus Christ of Nazareth, He [Christ the Messiah] is from the line of David. Even the blind uttered this [Mark 10: 47]. This son of God [David] carries DNA that makes him [David], the father of the Son [Jesus Christ]. We [sons of God] must allow God to live in and through us to father [influence] generations. Let us look at Ezra:

Ezra 7:6 *(ESV)*
This Ezra went up from Babylonia. He was a scribe skilled in the Law of Moses that the Lord, the God of Israel, had given, and the king granted him all that he asked, for the hand of the Lord his God was on him.

As I studied Ezra, I realised that from Aaron, the chief priest, to Eleazar, to Phinehas, to Abishua, to Bukki, to Uzzi, to Zerahiah, to Meraioth, to Azariah, to Amariah, to Ahitub, to Zadok, to Seraiah and finally Ezra, there are fourteen generations between Aaron, the chief priest and Ezra. While the natural thought would be that with each generation, there was a wealth of experience and increase in the measure of relationship with God; the sad reality is that there were peaks and troughs. In the Bible, the number fourteen implies a double measure of spiritual perfection; it also represents deliverance or salvation.

Is it possible that information of the nation of Israel's experience would have been relayed through the generations? Information such as slavery in Egypt, God's deliverance and exodus, the victories over various nations and the occupation of the promise land. I am sure as Ezra studied, he would have also looked at how the children of God would have deteriorated and fallen to such depths. In his day and time, Israel had sunk back into "slavery". They were in captivity. Instead of being under God's rulership, they were in Babylon. Babylon was ruling most of the known world, and God's people were now also its subjects. Babylon was the mother of all sin. It was such a secular system which consumed all in its path; anything and everything unimaginable was happening in Babylon. You were beaten into conformity with temptation and all the pleasures the world could give. It took a real man to stand up and take on the whole system and defy it. Ezra was a non-conformist. He did not read the script and decided to pursue the acts of his forefather, Aaron.

It is recorded that he was a skilled scribe in the five books of Moses. Skill speaks of training, being diligent, hard graft, putting in effort and application of oneself. This skill was not genetically transmitted and conveyed to him. He must have decided to be transformed by the Word of God from the inside out. Ezra decided not to defile himself with the practices or the teachings of Babylon. His mind was set; his desire was to see the will of God for his life and to lead his people once again, as Moses and his forefather Aaron had done. Warnings of past mistakes would have also been highlighted, and I am sure

Miriam would have also been spoken of. Ezra got God's attention. He drew near to God, and God responded.

Aaron and Hur held up the hands of Moses till sunset and God wrought a mighty victory for the children of Israel. Fourteen generations later, a descendant of Aaron, Ezra would open his mouth, and the most powerful king on earth would listen and grant him all that he requested for the children of Israel. I am certain that the easy way would have been to just be another face in the crowd—just to be another number, a casualty of captivity, a statistic and victim. It would have been easy to just wallow in self-pity and die blaming the state of affairs to the preceding generations. Instead, he read of Moses' refusal to be called a son of Pharaoh's daughter, and Ezra, too, refused to be Babylon's son. As a child in God's House, will you refuse to just be ordinary and be a son of this world?

Exodus 20: 5 - 6
You shall not bow down to them or serve them, for I the Lord your God am a jealous God, visiting the iniquity of the fathers on the children to the third and the fourth generation of those who hate me but showing steadfast love to thousands of generations to those who love me and keep my commandments.

The more mature in Christ I have become, I have realised that I appreciate my Heavenly Father more, which has also translated into a closer relationship now with my earthly father. This has also positively changed the respect I have for the spiritual leaders, who will one day give an account to God. If ever you mess up with your earthly parents, your pastor or mentor, don't be too proud to run back and ask for forgiveness. When tough seasons come, after we have been doing things our way, our first instinct must always be to turn to the Father. Like the prodigal [Luke 11], we must go back to our parents, pastors, or mentors to re-calibrate and reset. My encouragement to you is "be reconciled".

I am reminded of the story in Genesis 26: 18 - 26 of Isaac digging *again*, the wells he had dug with his father [Abraham]. When we read this story, we are reminded of how continuity and momentum can easily be lost. From this story, as children in the House of God, we should inherit from our fathers, live 'well-watered' lives, build on those platforms that have been laid by our predecessors and then in-turn, pass on to our own children or those that follow behind us [from Abraham to Isaac and then Jacob]. It was never part of the Father's original design for us to neglect, lose our ways, get distracted and derailed and then return to dig up our father's wells—again. Isaac went and dug his father's wells. He was starting all over again. By so doing, Isaac went back to elementary truths. When you come back to the Father, you will initially be fed milk [1 Peter 2: 2] in order to restore and strengthen you again. However, for those children in the House that have remained strong in the Lord, they will move from strength to strength and will graduate from milk to meat [Hebrews 5: 12 - 14]. Let us be completely sold out and pursue maturity, so that we become fully formed into the image of Jesus Christ the Son of God.

WARNING: BREAK IN CONTINUITY

II Timothy 4: 9 – 11

*Make every effort to come to me soon; for **Demas loved this world, has deserted me and has gone** to Thessalonica. Crescens has gone to Galatia and Titus to Dalmatia. Only Luke is with me. Get Mark and bring him with you, for he is very helpful to me for the ministry.*

I Chronicles 28: 9

*And Solomon, my son, get to know the God of your ancestors. Worship and serve Him with your whole heart and with a willing mind. For the Lord sees every heart and understands and knows every plan and thought. If you seek Him, you will find Him. **But if you forsake Him, He will reject you forever.***

To break is to separate or cause the separation of something into two or more pieces. A break can be deliberate, by mistake or purely out of ignorance. It can also be because of pressure from within or externally. Furthermore, a break can also be experienced suddenly or gradually.

Can you imagine starting a running race and deliberately not getting to the finish line? As you run you take your eyes off the prize ahead [Jesus]. You get drawn, distracted, derailed, or discouraged by your surrounds. Your running becomes a speed walk, then a gentle stroll, a stop, then you walk off the track, and you eventually have a desire to leave the track and stadium. This regression can be immediate or deceptively subtle. Provided you are in the arena on the track, the crowd in the grandstand won't stop chanting and urging you on [Hebrews 12: 1]. Even when you are determined to exit the arena, or oblivious, the crowd continue to scream, "Go back! Don't quit! You can do it!" The chanting continues and never stops, as it is only reserved for those who are participating. Sadly, as you continue walking away, the once upon a time vociferous decibels fade into a whisper, until there is absolute silence, as you eventually become tone deaf. Before you know it, you will discover yourself outside the arena swallowed and camouflaged by your sphere [Psalm 1: 1]. However, there is One who never stops pursuing you, by His Holy Spirit. He is the good Father who will keep the gate of the arena open for you. His Son Jesus Christ, who is our Lord and Saviour stands at the arena gate arms open wide, longing and desperate for your return. The power to return lies solely with you.

The question is not about whether you start or how you start. The question is: Can you finish what God has initiated through you? For example, can you imagine if you were travelling on a bus, and you came across an able bodied 20-year-old man or woman of sound-mind, who was still being bottle or breast-fed [like a baby]? A man or woman with adult incisors, premolars, and molars, yet being fed on milk and not solids. How would you react? I hope most of us would warn all concerned parties. As ridiculous as it sounds, I want to tell you that nowadays, so many things go unchecked, even in the Church. Maturity, progress, and continuity must be pursued by us all. For example, both of my parents were born in rural huts, and when they matured and progressed, I was in an urban clinic. I too made strides, as both my kids children were born in a modern hospital. Whilst I have used natural examples, I am here to tell you that primarily spiritually the Church must mature, progress, and continue.

It would be irresponsible of me if I did not warn you, just as Jesus did [Matthew 16: 6]. We need to be on guard against the yeast of some men and women, who are walking disorderly [II Thessalonians 3: 6]. Their exterior portrays images of holiness, and yet inside they are dead. They have a form of godliness, and yet in reality, deny and resist the power of God [II Timothy 3: 5]. These people are building on self and aim to fulfil selfish ambitions. They are so deceptive and seek to satisfy their big egos, fuel their 'superstar' status, and pursue titles. Such are they who impart and keep the Body of Christ immature and confused.

In his letter to Timothy, [2 Timothy 4: 9 - 11] Paul was concerned at the situation. The younger people [Demas] who were expected to carry the flame of the gospel were falling away. Such was his concern that he wrote to his son Timothy, urging him to come and see him quickly. He urged Timothy to bring Mark as Paul wanted to impart some spiritual wisdom. In addition, when you read David's words to Solomon [I Chronicles 28: 9], you get the impression that this is a father urging a son to walk with God in a greater measure than he did. He finishes off his words with a warning: 'If you don't take heed of my words, God will cut you off, forever!' [paraphrased]. A break in continuity means that momentum is lost, and it disrupts the flow, the health, and the state of the Church.

In Exodus 15: 26 and Deuteronomy 28: 1, simply put, God says, 'Live according to My statutes, and all that I have said over you will come to pass.' The flip side is if you don't, God will turn away from you and you will die. We must take Him seriously at His Word. Remember, we must fulfil our part. For example, if a parent has promised future payment of all university fees for a child currently in high school, it is clearly conditional. High school education must be completed and results that qualify and grant the child entry into university must be obtained. If the child does not fulfil the elementary or primary stage and fails entry into university, the parent cannot suddenly pay their money to the university to fulfill the commitment. The failure is not the parent but the child. I want to get into greater detail about some individuals who broke the flow and highlight the result that followed.

Leviticus 10: 1 - 11 (AMP)
Nadab and Abihu, the sons of Aaron, each took his censer and put fire in it, and put incense on it, and offered strange and unholy fire before the Lord, as He had not commanded them. And there came forth fire from before the Lord and killed them, and they died before the Lord. Then Moses said to Aaron, "This is what the Lord meant when He said, 'I [and My will, not their own] will be acknowledged as hallowed by those who come near Me, and before all the people I

will be honoured '." And Aaron said nothing. Moses called Mishael and Elzaphan, sons of Uzziel uncle of Aaron, and said to them, "Come near; carry your brethren from before the sanctuary out of the camp. So, they drew near and carried them in their under tunics [stripped of their priestly vestments] out of the camp, as Moses had said. And Moses said to Aaron and Eleazar and Ithamar, his sons [the father and brothers of the two priests whom God had slain for offering false fire], "Do not uncover your heads or let your hair go loose or tear your clothes, lest you die [also] and lest God's wrath should come upon all the congregation; but let your brethren, the whole house of Israel, bewail the burning which the Lord has kindled. And you shall not go out from the door of the Tent of Meeting, lest you die, for the Lord's anointing oil is upon you. And they did according to Moses' word." And the Lord said to Aaron, "Do not drink wine or strong drink, you or your sons, when you go into the Tent of Meeting, lest you die; it shall be a statute forever in all your generations. You shall make a distinction and recognize a difference between the holy and the common or unholy, and between the unclean and the clean; And you are to teach the Israelites all the statutes which the Lord has spoken to them by Moses."

I Samuel 2: 27 - 34 (AMP)

A man of God came to Eli and said to him, "Thus has the Lord said: I plainly revealed Myself to the house of your father [forefather Aaron] when they were in Egypt in bondage to Pharaoh's house Moreover, I selected him out of all the tribes of Israel to be My priest, to offer on My altar, to burn incense, to wear an ephod before Me. And I gave [from then on] to the house of your father [forefather] all the offerings of the Israelites made by fire. Why then do you kick [trample upon, treat with contempt] My sacrifice and My offering which I commanded and honour your sons above Me by fattening yourselves upon the choicest part of every offering of My people Israel? Therefore, the Lord, the God of Israel, says, I did promise that your house and that of your father [forefather Aaron] should go in and out before Me forever." But now the Lord says, "Be it far from Me. For those who honour Me,

*I will honour, and those who despise Me shall be lightly esteemed. Behold, the time is coming when I will cut off your strength and the strength of your own father's house, that there shall not be an old man in your house. And you shall behold the distress of My house, even in all the prosperity which God will give Israel, and there shall not be an old man in your house forever. Yet I will not cut off from My altar every man of yours; some shall survive to weep and mourn [over the family's ruin], **but all the increase of your house shall die in their best years. And what befalls your two sons, Hophni and Phinehas shall be a sign to you in one day; they both shall die.**" [Fulfilled in I Sam. 4:17, 18.]*

Please allow me to link these two stories to properly show you how continuity, legacy, and inheritance were disrupted. What Aaron witnessed and experienced must have been heart wrenching. God killed His sons on the same day [please take note, it was God who killed them]. Aaron was not to mourn but to carry on with life like all other days. His sons' bodies were taken in the equivalent of our modern-day underwear—how undignified. Word must have travelled throughout Israel: 'The High Priest's sons have been killed by God!' Fear must have come upon the nation that God is not to be insulted or ridiculed. I am convinced that this information would have been passed down through the generations by Aaron's descendants. However, in a subsequent generation, Eli, a descendant of Ithamar [Numbers 3: 2 & I Samuel 2: 27] the youngest son of *Aaron*, also had two sons who committed the *same* offence. Eli either completely did not know how God treated Aaron's sons, or he was very ignorant and arrogant. Somewhere along the line, there was no transfer of experience. In fact, Eli's sons did not make a distinction or recognise the difference between the holy and the common; they did not reverentially fear God. As a result, God also killed Eli and his sons on the same day [once again take note, it was God who killed them].

It appears that no one taught Hophni and Phinehas, all the statutes which the Lord had spoken. They were given titles that they never measured up to. They probably did not have the character nor the anointing. They followed in the footsteps of their near relatives Nadab and Abihu. The result was the same—premature death. In one generation, God killed Nabal and Abihu, but in the following generation, God took it to the next level; He killed the father too and ensured that there would be no continuity of "a faulty gene" in His house—this is serious. In I Kings 2: 27, Solomon expelled Abiathar from being a priest to the Lord, thus fulfilling the word of the Lord spoken concerning the house of Eli in Shiloh. This action was not a generational curse; it was simply a lack of total surrender, understanding or fully embracing the mantle of God. We need to realise that even in our day, there are things God is going to kill for the sake of seeing a mature Church.

Eli had qualified to his office on hereditary grounds; his DNA could be traced back to Aaron. He had deficiencies; he did not internalise, undergo character assassination or a detailed examination of self. Could it be possible that he did not know about Aaron's experience and the death of his sons? We must teach others all the statutes of the Lord, telling them of our experiences and warning them of the consequences of not walking in His precepts. Let us not break the flow. Instead, pass on experience, of successes, errors, and mistakes. There is no room to hide things which may become cyclical in the next generation. Let our experience make it easier for the coming generations to deal with events, situations, and incidences. Let us make it easier for them to walk in the authentic and tangible things of God.

FAILURE OF A COUNTRY OR NATION

Exodus 1:8- 10 (KJV)
Now there arose up a new king over Egypt, which knew not Joseph and he said unto his people, Behold, the people of the children of Israel are more and mightier than we: Come on, let us deal wisely with them; lest they multiply, and it come to pass, that, when there

falleth out any war, they join also unto our enemies, and fight against us, and so get them up out of the land.

Years before this new King arose, described in Genesis 41, Egypt had become the world's focal point as drought and famine had ravaged every nation on earth. People from every tongue and tribe flocked to purchase grain and foodstuffs from Egypt. The availability of food in Egypt was because of Joseph [a Hebrew], who walked with and knew God. It is human nature to be puffed up and arrogant. I am convinced that the Egyptians would have been bursting with pride, as being the envy of the world. They lived in plush luxury and abundance while the rest of the world struggled. Egypt was a superpower, a nation to be admired and feared. If this were in our modern world, Egypt's veto or approval would have been obeyed by any nation. Like begets like, and unfortunately, the "seed" of image or self would have filtered through the Egyptian generations, which bore fruit that would eventually became the nation's downfall.

Let me highlight a couple of things that took place before Joseph's promotion. The king who elevated Joseph knew that Joseph was a Hebrew. Pharaoh therefore knew that this was a culture clash, as well as a difference in worship or religion. Pharaoh overlooked these differences. When Pharaoh promoted Joseph from prison to Prime Minister of Egypt, I suggest to you that even the historians of the nation would have documented this. Joseph's name, origins, and his God had to appear in the records. I want to highlight further that the drought that had obliterated the world in those years and forced the world to come to Egypt in search of food would also have been documented. Once again, Joseph's name would have been recorded high on the list. God through Joseph kept Egypt from harm, as well as spared the then known world.

How does it follow that a king arises and not know Joseph [Exodus 1: 8]? History tells us that it is the Egyptians that invented paper from papyrus. Surely, there were parchments stored somewhere with this information. The king during Joseph's Day would have passed these records on. Every king would have had advisers and historians. Somewhere along the line, someone either deliberately misinformed this new king destroyed records, or through ignorance, this new king did not refer to history. Fast forward, this is what happened.

Exodus 11: 5 - 6 (AMP)
All the firstborn in the land [the pride, hope, and joy] of Egypt shall die, from the firstborn of Pharaoh, who sits on his throne, even to the firstborn of the maidservant who is behind the handmill, and all the firstborn of beasts. There shall be a great cry in all the land of Egypt such as has never been nor ever shall be again.

The same God who spared the nation of Egypt in one generation is the same who, in another generation, killed the firstborn of every creature in Egypt: human and beasts. The first-born child represented the son, the rightful heir in any household. A firstborn is a symbol of continuity, the pride, hope, and joy of any home. On this particular day, Egypt lost its heir to the throne, and the population witnessed the death of *all* firstborns. Suddenly, Egypt begged Moses and Israel to leave. As a result of a lack of continuity, the country that once blossomed, during the time of Joseph, was now in mourning the death of every first born. Can you imagine the mass graves, carcasses everywhere, and the nauseating stench? The site would have been gloomy, bleak, and off-putting. Rather than attracting foreign nations to itself, Egypt was now a country to stay away from. The once glorious nation which drew populations would have been the last place on earth anyone would have wanted to visit.

There is a possibility that this king would have been from a long dynasty, a son of a former king. He did not catch the vision established by his forefather who set Joseph as second in charge of Egypt. The king who invited Israel into Egypt realised that without the children of Israel [through Joseph], the earth could have perished due to hunger. Someone did not think and act generationally. As a result, a whole generation [firstborns] in Egypt was wiped off the face of the earth.

God means business, even in our day. How dare we live for ourselves, just for this era and time. Is the fault with fathers or with the sons? Is the responsibility solely with parents or is it two ways? Have we done enough to ensure that things are taken to the very core of the next generations' lives? Do they value and know how to handle the things of God? Have we made every effort to pass on detail, or are we about to lose generations?

FAILURE OF FUTURE LEADERS IN GOD'S HOUSE

II Kings 2: 3 & 5 (AMP)
3: The prophets' sons who were at Bethel came to Elisha and said, "Do you that the Lord will take your master away from you today?" He said, "Yes, I know; hold your peace."
5: The sons of the prophets who were at Jericho came to Elisha and said, "Do you know that the Lord will take your master away from you today?" And he answered, "Yes, I know it; hold your peace."

Notice how these sons of prophets were very cerebral and had the revelation of things to come and yet did nothing? It is evident to me that these sons were probably spoilt. They wanted the image and titles as people with prophetic insight, but they did not live it out. They preferred the praises and recognition of man; they got the attention from people but clearly did not interpret the times and failed to question God: What God was doing, and why was He doing it? What became of each of them? What will become of you? In Elijah they had a model and teacher, and each of them was born to a parent, and therefore should have been trained to be well-rounded. Instead, Elisha the servant of the Prophet Elijah succeeded as the Prophet. What will become of you? Have you grasped that Kingdom Leadership has always been servant leadership? Consider Jesus Christ.

As the Body of Christ, let's go beyond just being seen, to being authentic and real. The sons of prophets are incomparable, are no match and not worthy of mention when we think of Joseph [Genesis]. When Joseph interpreted pharaoh's dream; from the revelation from

God, there came wisdom and application. Joseph also gave the king of Egypt a solution [see Genesis 41: 33-36]. 'Do not merely listen to the word, and so deceive yourselves. Do what it says [James 1: 22]. Simply because your parents or mentors are on fire for God, that does not make you of equal standing. You are going to have to be that sacrifice on the altar in order for God to use you. Die to self and then walk with God daily.

FAILURE OF THE NEXT GENERATION

II Kings 2: 23-25 (NIV)
From there Elisha went up to Bethel. As he was walking along the road, some youths came out a town and jeered at him, "Go on up, you baldhead!" they said. He turned round, looked at them then called down a curse on them in the name of the Lord. Then two bears came out of the woods and mauled forty-two of the youths. And he went on to Mount Carmel and from there returned to Samaria.

Stupidity or ignorance unfortunately is inexcusable in the eyes of God. You may know friends, colleagues, or family who have provoked God. Death will come upon some people we know. We must act and get them saved. After the above incident, a couple of parents were in mourning. Can you imagine forty-two youths being mauled to death? A generation in forty-two households was obliterated; potential was lost. The deceased either did not know God, did not love God or even treated God as common. They could have been related or were just bad friends misleading each other. Bad company corrupts good character [I Corinthians 15: 33]. Who is to blame? Was it the parents' failure to teach, impart, and reinforce? Was it the youths' deliberate lack of interest? Was it their disobedience or simply ignorance? Whatever conclusion we draw up will not change the fact that they jeered Elisha the Prophet. Somewhere along the line, they should have known to respect their elders—reverential fear of God. Anything short of this would lead to serious consequences. A lesson is clearly demonstrated by young David, who would not even 'touch' King Saul, God's anointed, even when Saul was in error [I Chronicles 16: 22]. Does the next generation truly know God's delegated authority? Do they understand honour's reward? Do they know respect?

FAILURE OF SERVANTS IN THE HOUSE OF GOD

In my mind, Elisha would have wanted to continue and establish the trend that had been triggered by his master Elijah. He recruited Gehazi as a servant, just as he too had been summoned as a servant. Elisha knew that the way to go up is go down—die to self. He knew the deep places one had to go for God to shape you. He knew that obscurity did not mean rejection by God. Just as he had learned, can I suggest, that perhaps Elisha wanted to ensure that vision would be caught by Gehazi, and continuity birthed. It is clear that Elisha had a longing for Gehazi to desire the anointing of God in a way he [Elisa] had.

The meaning of the name Gehazi is 'a valley of vision'. What a contradiction. He had a name with deep meaning, he lived daily with the prophet Elisha, God positioned him, and yet he still missed God's vision. Instead, we see in Gehazi, a young man who, once again, was after creating an image, an identity and self-recognition. He wanted the riches and fame but did not want to drink from the same cup the man of God had drunk from. Clearly, Gehazi was not cut from the same cloth as Elisha. He represents a generation who want to be seen at the top without having done any work; a generation that wants things done now and not later, those who lack patience, those who want the fire but do not have the oil to keep the flame alive [Matthew 25: 1 - 13]. People whose identity is only by association to the authentic and, yet in themselves, will not enter in and do the works of Christ. Have you ever been around people who talk up their spiritual parents, their parents, their church leaders, or mentors, and yet in themselves have never witnessed to anyone or even laid hands on a sick fly? I believe Gehazi was that type of person:

***II Kings 8: 4 - 5** (The Message Bible)*

The king was talking with Gehazi, servant to the Holy Man, saying, "Tell me some stories of the great things Elisha did." It so happened that as he was telling the king the story of the dead person brought back to life, the woman whose son was brought to life showed up asking for her home and farm. Gehazi said, "My master the king, this is the woman! And this is her son whom Elisha brought back to life!"

I am convinced that Elisha would have taught, counselled, and perhaps even disciplined Gehazi countless times. On one occasion, Gehazi's ill-discipline went a step too far, and his spiritual father [Elisha] realized that this 'son' was never going to change and measure up to the calling of God. Have you noticed that it is, the outward or image, and status that Gehazi always took pride in? Image is what God used to discipline him—he became leprous for all to see:

***II Kings 5: 15 - 16; 20; 22; 25; 26 - 27** (KJV)*

15: And he [Naaman - emphasis] returned to the man of God, he and all his company, and came, and stood before him [Elijah]: and he said, "Behold, now I know that there is no God in all the earth, but in Israel: now therefore, I pray thee, take a blessing of thy servant."

16: But he [Elisha] said, "As the LORD liveth, before whom I stand, I will receive none." And he [Naaman] urged him to take it, but he [Elisha] refused.

20: But Gehazi, the servant of Elisha the man of God, said, "Behold, my master hath spared Naaman this Syrian, in not receiving at his hands that which he brought: but, as the LORD liveth, I will run after him, and take somewhat of him."

22: And he [Gehazi] said, "All is well. My master hath sent me, saying, 'Behold, even now there be come to me from mount Ephraim two young men of the sons of the prophets: give them, I pray thee, a talent of silver, and two changes of garments'."

25: But he [Gehazi] went in and stood before his master. And Elisha said unto him, "Whence comest thou, Gehazi?" And he said, "Thy servant went no whither."

26: And he [Elisha] said unto him [Gehazi], "Went not mine heart with thee when the man turned again from his chariot to meet thee? Is it a time to receive money and to receive garments, and olive yards, and vineyards, and sheep, and oxen, and menservants, and maidservants?"

27: The leprosy therefore of Naaman shall cleave unto thee, and unto thy seed forever. And he went out from his presence a leper as white as snow.

One selfish act by Gehazi not only destroyed one man but generations. Continuity was immobilised. Remember, you have a representative responsibility. One slip up by you will destroy generations to follow. In these last days, God will not allow anyone to get away with nonsense. Gehazi's short-sightedness and desire to make easy money turned out to be his downfall. He loved money more than he feared God. His actions were immature, childish, and self-centred. He focused on self and failed to realise that he was a seed carrier.

FAILURE OF THOSE IN POLITICAL AUTHORITY

Proverbs 21: 1

The king's heart is in the hand of the Lord; as rivers of water, He turns it wherever He will.

I Timothy 2: 1 - 4

I urge then, first of all, that petitions, prayers, intercessions and thanksgiving be made for all people—for kings and all those in authority that we may live peaceful and quiet lives in all godliness and holiness. This is good and pleases God our Saviour.

Even kings, presidents, prime ministers, and political leaders, if not in tune with God can derail a whole nation, if the Church does nothing. Did you know that the Bible says 'The heart of a king [country leader] is the hands of God, and just like the rivers, He steers these leaders wherever He will' [Proverbs 21]? Furthermore, in his letter to Timothy, Paul encouraged that the Church pray for those in authority, that we may live quiet and peaceful lives so that the gospel of Jesus Christ be preached unreservedly [1Timothy 2]. When you combine these two passages [Proverbs & I Timothy], you will see that Church is the most powerful entity on earth. For God to steer, the Church *must* act and pray. Be on the lookout for my other Book, *Unrestrained Devotion—essential prayer ingredients*, where we discuss prayer. Remember, God moves in a nation because the Church is praying:

II Chronicles 7: 14

If my people, who are called by name [the Church, the Body of Christ, Christians - my emphasis] will humble themselves and pray and seek my face and turn from their wicked ways, then I will hear from Heaven, and I will forgive their sin and will heal their land [their country or Nation].

Let's look at the Word and see some failings by some who were in authority. At the coronation of Saul as the "first king" of Israel, Samuel highlighted that he was now old and that his sons were available for the nation of Israel, to consult [I Samuel 12]. It is clear to me that Samuel was clearly handing the baton to his sons, for the sake of continuity. He desired that Israel move from strength to strength. Not long after his coronation, Saul led the nation downhill, and it is also apparent that Samuel's sons did not carry the same anointing as he did. Samuel's words to Saul concerning rebellion being as sin of witchcraft [I Samuel 15: 23] came into manifestation when Samuel was dead. In his distress, Saul asked a medium to raise Samuel from the dead [I Samuel 28], 'for the word of the Lord was scarce, either by the prophets [Samuel's sons], or even dreams. The medium summoned the spirit of Samuel, who was not pleased with being summoned, and went on to confirm the disaster that would fall on the nation of Israel, as well as the death of Saul and his sons.

Continuity broke at spiritual leadership level, political leadership level, national level, and at individual level, leading to a disastrous period.

In addition, when you read the story of Gideon [Judges 6: 12 - 40; 7: 1 - 25] and observe how God brought victory over the armies of Midian, Amalek, and people from the east, it is sad to note that an alliance once existed between Midianites and Israelites. Midianites were also descendants of Abraham [who was also the father of Israel]. Moses, a leader of Israel married Zipporah, a Midianite [Exodus 2]. However, 200 years after the death of Moses, Israel defeated Midian—an absolute massacre and annihilation. Continuity ceased in one generation, and as a result, the two groups were at war Blood was shed, and people died. In our day, the most powerful entity on earth is not a particular nation, or a particular political leader, it's not a particular race [although some think they are] and neither is it a corporation. The most powerful entity is the Church—the Body of Christ.

The Church should no longer just sit idle or echo the same sentiments as the world in blaming the politicians for the state of affairs in any nation. The Church must take an inward look. We must look in the mirror. God wants to heal every nation; He wants the Church or Body of Christ to ask Him. He wants us to pray for our political leaders, so that He directs them, just like flowing water in a river can easily be directed. He will steer those in authority. We need to be telling our Father what we desire in the nations—primarily, for quiet peaceful lives, so that we may influence every sphere for Jesus Christ—birthing continuity. When the Church does nothing, the leaders cast off restraint, and similarly, the citizens follow. Continuity ceases, and God is left to start all over again!

This curtain is fast coming to a close, and we are in the end times. Whilst things get tough, rough, and topsy-turvy, the Church's primary mission of making disciples—continuity—must *never* stop. We are to petition God, and we are to invoke God. We must pray! Here is my question to every Christian, every Church: Is there a correlation between what is going on in your country with the level, frequency and sincerity of your prayers and petitions? Do you regularly pray for those in authority, your government and political leaders? Or do you only turn to prayer in crisis?

Let me conclude this chapter with Paul's warning; continuity does not mean, just appointing anyone for appointing's sake. Leaders in the Body of Christ must not be novices or recent converts, or else they might be conceited and fall under the same judgement as the devil. [I Timothy 3: 6]. Appointing someone is a time of transmission and transition. It is a time when we need to get prophetic. One mistake by the one handing over or the one receiving, can derail the kingdom. It is better to wait on God, than to run ahead of Him. We cannot afford to move forward without the unction of the Holy Ghost. Psalm 127: 1 - As long as we allow God to build the House, we will not break the continuity. Have you ever noticed that in that verse, people still build something, but without God – in vain? Make sure you have heard from God before handing over the baton to a novice, or else you will destroy what God has initiated in you.

A LASTING LEGACY

Job 19: 23 -24

Oh, that my words were written! Oh, that they were inscribed in a book! Oh, that with an iron pen and lead they were engraved in the rock forever!

II Peter 1: 13 – 15

I think it is right, as long as I am in this body, to stir you up by way of reminder since I know that the putting off of my body will be soon, as our Lord Jesus Christ made clear to me and I will make every effort, so that after my departure you may be able at any time to recall these things.

We have already defined legacy and inheritance earlier in this book. In the above verses, Job and Peter mean business. Job wanted his words written down for encouragement, instruction, warning and ultimately to show God's unwavering love. He did not want it written on anything flimsy that would rot, decompose and be discarded; he wanted rocks as the material. He did not want it inked with something that could easily be erased. He wanted it penned with iron and lead, and to be engraved in a rock. One of the characteristics of lead is that it is very resistant to corrosion. Job was interested in permanence! His legacy was to outlive him – and it certainly happened, as we celebrate his faithfulness toward God, even today. Peter later desired to stir you and I up, and as he is now dead and present with God for eternity, we remember his very words and actions. 'After my departure, I want you to recall the goodness of our Lord Jesus Christ' [paraphrased]. Peter was simply saying to each of us, don't forget the Message. I also love what John said in his epistle, "I have no greater joy than to hear that my children walk in truth" [III John 1: 4].

Each of us can influence others for eternity. What is passed on, handed down, or transmitted can be something physical, and it can also be spiritual, or something intangible. We have faith, wisdom, knowledge, experiences, relationships, dreams, vision, ideas, plans, aspirations, and/or assets to pass on. Our influence must outlive our physical existence. Instead of building personal empires, personal reputations, and names, we must extend God's Kingdom. All who are in Christ, who walk with and die in Him, must influence this world for perpetuity. When our exit draws near, the state of the Body of Christ, our families and sphere, must be in a healthier, and stronger state than when we found them. We are like a tree branch or Aaron's staff. We defy all logic and bear fruit. In nature if a branch is slashed from a tree, it results in death for the branch. Not so, of Aaron's staff, it blossoms and still produces fruit—almonds! [Numbers 17: 2, 8]. Remember, Jesus is the vine, and we are the branches [John 15: 5]. If we remain grafted in Him, we will bear much fruit.

As royal priesthoods [I Peter 2: 9] continuing from where Aaron left, let us, understand that God is our inheritance. In Numbers 18:20, God said to Aaron, "You priests will receive no inheritance of land or share of property among the people of Israel. I am your inheritance and your share." This is also directed at us, at our children, and subsequent generations. If we neglect this truth and knowledge, the result will be catastrophic. In Hosea 4: 6, God said, 'My people are being destroyed because they don't know Me. It is your entire fault, you priests, for you yourselves refuse to know Me. Now I refuse to recognize you as My priests. Since you have forgotten the laws of your God, I will forget to bless your children.' We need to recognise that our negative actions or inactivity can affect generations too.

You are never too young or too old to pass on something. Like Abraham and Sarah, you have Isaac in you [Genesis 18], like Moses I believe God is asking the same question, 'What is that you have in your hand?' [Exodus 4: 2 - 5]. Who you are and what you have is God's starting point with you. You may suppose you are in the twilight of life, that you have a speech impediment or that you have little oil in a jar, but God sees a son of promise for you to impact. He sees an orator who will stand before kings and He sees business ideas that can save generations. It is this legacy that we are being confronted with to leave. The biggest investment you and I can make is not the purchase of houses or land, stocks and shares, gilts, or bonds, but the pouring of self; Christ in you passed on, to live in and through the coming generations. It is investing in people, the passing on of the spiritual: faith, dreams, visions, plans, ideas, and experiences.

A generation must glow and be infectious, rather than being too hot that it burns, scolds, and damages. What we carry and have must not end with us. As our flame turns into ember, it must ignite others, so that there is definite continuity. We need to believe in the next generation, just as God does. Some have been frightened about what the future holds for their children and their children's children. I am fully persuaded that as this curtain draws nigh, the coming generations will be a more mature Church, growing incrementally in starture, holiness, and godliness. The power of our tongues must echo in future generations as our words of life reverberate. We need to provide the match sticks and fuel, so that future generations fan into flame the gifts of God that are residing in them. Let us be so resolute in this quest and be determined that our encouragement converts potential into realisation.

Numbers 11: 14 - 17, 24 - 30 (NLT)
14 – 17: I can't carry all these people by myself! The load is far too heavy! If this is how you intend to treat me, just go ahead and kill me. Do me a favour and spare me this misery!" Then the Lord said to Moses, "Gather before me seventy men who are recognised as elders and leaders of Israel. Bring them to the tabernacle to stand there with you. I will come down and talk to you there. I will take some of the Spirit that is upon you, and I will put the Spirit upon them also. They will bear the burden of the people along with you, so you will not have to carry it alone...
24 – 30: So Moses went out and reported the Lord's words to the people. He gathered the seventy elders and stationed them around the

tabernacle, and the Lord came down in the cloud and spoke to Moses. **Then he gave the seventy elders the same Spirit that was upon Moses.** *And when the Spirit rested upon them, they prophesied. But this never happened again. Two men, Eldad and Medad, had stayed behind in the camp. They were listed among the elders, but they had not gone out to the tabernacle. The Spirit rested upon them as well, so they prophesied there in the camp. A young man ran and reported to Moses, "Eldad and Medad are prophesying in the camp!" Joshua, son of Nun, who had been Moses' assistant since his youth, protested, "Moses, my master, make them stop!" But Moses replied, "Are you jealous for my sake? I wish that all the Lord's people were prophets and that the Lord would put his Spirit upon them all!" Then Moses returned to the camp with the elders of Israel.*

In the Book of Numbers, Moses openly confesses to God that he cannot carry the people alone. He does not want to be seen as the man for the hour, neither does he want the popularity vote. Moses is not bothered with the prominent man of God status and clearly does not want the celebrity status. He is not the latest craze and is not seeking recognition as the man of God with a congregation of 1.5 million members. His desire is to please God, but he also knows his limitations. Moses is not jealous; he is not prideful, nor does he sulk or suddenly want to change his mind about leading the Hebrew nation when God suggests that He will put the same Spirit that was upon him and make other leaders. Moses is not belittling himself. God stands in agreement with Moses and this example teaches the Church, that we should impart to others for the sake of nourishment, vitality, and continuity. We also see the innocence of youth [Joshua] and the wisdom of experience [Moses]. Moses corrected Joshua's attitude, over Eldad and Medad. God *replicates* Moses; He does not *duplicate* him. God takes the exact same Spirit that is upon Moses and puts it on others—that is replication. God does not turn the other men into "*types*" of Moses' [imitate and follow a man's faith, but don't try and dress, walk and talk like anyone else]. Instead of having one anointed and Spirit filled man in the land, they were suddenly seventy-one.

The humility of Moses and his willingness to see others filled with the Holy Spirit was a foretaste of the New Testament Church – the whole Body of Christ being filled with the Spirit.

In Acts 17: 1 - 6, Paul and Silas, who had already turned the world upside down, entered Thessalonica and 'replicated' themselves. A significant number gave their lives to the Lord, both men and women. These two people stirred the city and left it with a bunch of bold, Holy Spirit filled and tongue talking citizens of the kingdom of God, who were passionate and determined to invade their spheres of influence and usher in the rulership of King Jesus. Let us ignite destiny, persuade holiness, encourage mission, and then boldly commission the next generation instructing them that, remaining rooted in God, one can chase a thousand, and two will put ten thousand to flight [Deuteronomy 32: 30].

Legacy is not reserved for the elect or esoteric, and it is not tied to birth right. Ordinary people like you and I have a choice of what to do with what we have, regardless of what life brings our way. Unlike the sons of the prophets, the servant Elisha a son of Shaphat understood the responsibility and accountability of a prophet. He saw the mantle upon Elijah the prophet as truly authentic and desired it. Realising that God would take Elijah, Elisha could not fathom the world without such a class of prophet. He earnestly desired the mantle of the prophet and just like the woman with the issue of blood [Luke 8], Elisha 'pressed' through the sons of the prophets. When questioned by Elijah about his desire, Elisha did not flinch or get scared even though his response seemed ridiculous:

II Kings 2: 9 *(NIV)*
When they had crossed, Elijah said to Elisha, "Tell me what can I do for you before I am taken away from you?" "Let me inherit a double portion of your spirit," Elisha replied.

He desired; he pursued and received a double portion of the anointing of God, so much so, that even the sons of the prophets recognised and acknowledged. Elisha had no physical prophetic genes in his lineage and furthermore rejected the taunts from the sons of the prophets. In a single day, God promoted Elisha from a servant to a prophet, just as generations before, God had promoted Joseph from prison to the palace. Any parent would have been proud to witness their son transition, from servant to prophet. Equally proud of Elisha would've been Elijah, the mentor, teacher, master, and father figure. I am sure Elijah tested his servant and eventually concluded in himself that God's kingdom would be safe in his protégé's hands. This relationship initially began as master-servant, and then evolved to teacher-student relationship. After all the testing of Elisha's heart and finding him pure in every way, Elijah drew a 'young' Elisha closer to himself and the relationship further metamorphosed to father-son. Children and the next generation must be tested. Do they have the right mental attitude? Do they have the calling, the gifting, and more importantly, the character? Do they have stickability, or do they whither when facing adversity and confrontation? Do they have a care and concern for others? Are they glory boys and girls, or do they glorify the One Whom all praise is due?

II Kings 2: 2, 4, 6 (ESV)
2: And Elijah said to Elisha, "Please stay here, for the Lord has sent me as far as Bethel." But Elisha said, "As the Lord lives, and as you yourself live, I will not leave you."4: Elijah said to him, "Elisha, please stay here, for the Lord has sent me to Jericho." But he said, "As the Lord lives, and as you yourself live, I will not leave you." So they came to Jericho.
6: Then Elijah said to him [Elisha], "Please stay here, for the Lord has sent me to the Jordan." But he said, "As the Lord lives, and as you yourself live, I will not leave you." So the two of them went on.

II Kings 2: 2, 4, 6 is another Peter, son of Jonah moment [John 21: 15 - 19]. Elijah was asking Elisha, "Yes, you have the calling. Yes, you have the character, but do you love God more than the sons of the prophets?" Elijah was going Home but certainly going to leave another to do the 'greater than these shall you do in my name, as I go away to my Father.' [John 14: 12]. Perish the thought that we would even consider the Church as diminishing.

In Hebrews 11: 4, it says that though Abel is dead, his blood still speaks. We are his heirs, we offer God a more excellent sacrifice daily, and we are imploring, pleading, and reasoning with others for the kingdom's sake. We are fixated and determined that no one is left without hearing, knowing, and running after this great and awesome God. Abel is long gone, and he lies in the hall of fame of the Book of Hebrews. His descendants are turning this world upside down. Those that feed off us must consume sufficiently; we must be infectious, contagious, create desire, stimulate action, and cause them to outlive themselves. We all need to realise that this is a God thing; it has never been and will never be any other thing.

I believe that we are living in times when God requires more from His Church. I think that things will be shaken in the heavens and here on earth. I believe God desires maturity; in fact, He is demanding maturity. I believe that God will kill attitudes, habits, and even people that have polluted His House, just as in the early days of the Church— Peter confronting Ananias and his wife Sapphira [Acts 5: 1 - 11]. I believe those that have turned their hearts to money, other priorities, and other gods above God shall have their hearts exposed for all to witness—just as Jesus did at the Temple in Jerusalem [Mark 11: 15 - 17]. The maturity of the Church is required; it is necessary. Jesus, the Groom, is not coming for an immature Bride. A groom of honour never marries one who is underage and immature. Let us be active, facilitate, prepare, and present this glorious Bride called the Church, positioning multiple generations, so that She attains her full stature. Let us break the cycle of starting and stopping, repeatedly. We need to ensure that the generations' grow from strength to strength until the Church is consuming meat [Hebrews 5: 12 - 14].

God never created us just to live ordinary lives; we were birthed to live supernaturally normal lifestyles—living the God kind of life.

This life is too short to waste it on unnecessary things. If the current status-quo of a lack of pro-activity remains, we would be foolish, arrogant, and no different from the previous generations who did not learn and impart their successes or warn of their failures. This would be insanity; repeating the same fruitless things and hoping that someday, by chance, it will eventually yield results. We must not tire in identifying individuals, discerning God's call of their respective function, and training them for their proper trades, so that they never backslide or leave. It is also important that every preceding generation constantly recruit, induct, demonstrate competency habits, as well as encourage excellence without a compromise on holiness and complete yieldedness to God. We must consider succession plans that instil increase, continuity, longevity, permanence, and eternity.

When this proactiveness becomes a lifestyle, the coming generations will consider their predecessors' thoughts and gleanings; they will read their records and accounts; they will learn, they will be empowered, and they will be catapulted into new levels and go on to do much more. As each of us initiate continuity, the pursuing generations will enter a Church that is firm and stable and cannot be shaken, offering God a pleasing service, acceptable worship with modesty and pious care, and Godly fear and awe—[Hebrews 12: 28] The early Church which began with twelve Apostles, and then grew initially by addition, then multiplication of Spirit-filled believers will in our generation and the coming generations quadruple, pentatriene, hexatriene, and then explode exponentially. Jesus is returning for the harvest of harvests.

In Luke 2: 22 - 38, in two separate incidents, Joseph and Mary heard, two very old people speak prophetically and confirm what they had heard. This would have removed any doubts if any had crept into Joseph. It would have affirmed that they were indeed fathering the Messiah. Both prophet Simeon who had waited to see the Messiah and prophet Anna [the daughter of Peneul, which means "face of God"] literally saw God in flesh. Simeon and Anna's legacy was their conveying to the people around them that Jesus is the Messiah. In old age, let our inner man be sharp, alert, attentive and effervescent. Let us be sober minded, dignified, self-controlled, sound in faith, in love and in steadfastness [Titus 2: 2]. Let's go out leaving a blaze of God's glory.

In Psalm 71: 18 when David was an old man he said, 'Now also when I am old and grey headed, O God, do not forsake me; until I have showed your strength to this generation, and your power to everyone that is to come [subsequent generations]'. In old age, David was not interested in retiring, just like in Psalm 92: 14, his desire was to bear fruit in old age and remain evergreen. That is how I want to be remembered—not just for the finances, houses, or land; I want to primarily leave a spiritual inheritance. Saints from every age will adore God when every preceding generation is inspired to establish God's Kingdom; run a good race, contribute, build a better future for the Church, and hold out the baton. Each successive generation should recognise that they are standing on the shoulders of giants who have gone before.

Isaiah 61: 7 – 8: Instead of your shame you will receive a double portion, and instead of disgrace you will rejoice in your inheritance, and so you will inherit a double portion in your land, and everlasting joy will be yours.

EPILOGUE

*Keep watch over yourselves and all the flock which the Holy Spirit has made you overseers. Be shepherds of the Church of God, which He bought with His own blood. [**Acts 20: 28 – NIV**]*

This was part of Paul's farewell letter to the Church at Ephesus. Upon scrutiny of the above verse, from the word "overseers," as well as the statement, "shepherds of the Church of God," you probably deduced that this part of the letter was directed mainly at elders and pastors. As a result, I know that generally most readers will want to shut their ears, exonerate, and excuse themselves from Paul's statement but please allow me to reason with you and highlight some things which are pertinent. Please flow with me, take away the title overseer and consider your own actions, because faith without works is dead. Let's focus on the expression "*watch over yourselves,*" as well as the word *overseer.* Although there is a distinct difference between the clergy and layperson, there is the unending truth that each of us need to also watch over ourselves in our manner of lives or *actions.* Undoubtedly, Paul was passionate about continuity and was stressing a point. Why? Because Man has the propensity to focus on self and be full of self-importance. Consider this, each of us has a sphere of influence and the responsibility for getting people saved, for modelling Christ, for mentoring and for leading people to maturity lies with each of us. This is because God has given every believer everything required for living a godly life [II Peter 1: 3].

Let me simplify further and bring home truths, as I believe that we can ALL learn from Paul's statement. Whilst Overseer is an office in the Church, the word *overseer* is derived from the word oversee. From the *actions* of the word oversee, we derive the word oversight. Coincidentally, the word oversight has two opposite meanings. One of the meanings is, the unintentional failure to notice or do something. The other meaning is the effective supervision of something. Although you may not be an Overseer within the Church, as a child of God [an individual or layperson], you have oversight of the people in your sphere [in the world]. As far as the kingdom of God is concerned, your oversight is one of two things—an unintentional failure, whereby people in your sphere are going to Hell even though you are there. Perhaps, you have never witnessed or thought to share the good news about Jesus Christ? Is today your reality check? Maybe you have been fruitless, even though God has strategically handpicked you and planted you in that ripe harvest field [your current sphere]. On the other hand, your oversight may be effective. You may already have triggered an eternal domino effect for eternity, to the glory of God.

Honestly assess yourself. How do you measure up against the Lord's continuity directive, of making disciples [Matthew 28: 19 – 20]? As believers, we all have oversight responsibilities [Mark 16: 15 – 16 & Acts 1: 8]. When people are born again, accept and follow the Lordship of Jesus Christ, and come into His Church, then they become the primary responsibility of the Overseer or local pastor—not yours [as per Paul's statement above]. However, we must still be in their lives, just like the early Church [read Acts 4: 34]. My very direct question is this: Which definition of oversight best describes you? Remember, you are either hot or cold – you cannot define yourself as part unintentional and partly effective. If you do, it is like calling yourself lukewarm. Heaven's expectation is that each of us must be red-hot. Psalm 105: 1 – 2 says, 'Give praise to the Lord [Jesus Christ] proclaim His name, make known among the nations what He has done. Sing to Him, sing praise to Him, tell of all His wonderful acts.' There is an urgency to make disciples, we need to snatch many out of the grip of a lost eternity, we need to continue and never tire. In the process of doing so, we refresh and recharge ourselves by giving Him ALL the glory.

Your effective oversight in your sphere today, will lead you into becoming tomorrow's Overseer in the Church. [Body of Christ Leadership]. Like Joseph [Genesis], today, you may be in prison, interpreting other prisoners' dreams, but tomorrow, you will be the

Prime Minister, leading a nation. You may even be like David [I Samuel], tending to sheep in the wilderness, but tomorrow a whole nation may look to you. I don't know whether you know it, but the Church does not have the luxury to stutter, fall, and then rise again, like any other entity or institution on earth. The Church of Jesus Christ is supposed to have a continuous conveyor belt of servant leadership, who are salt, light, and fruitful—past, present, and future! The Church should not lose any generation, and in *every* generation, the Body of Christ must know who will be in its future leadership— driving the same uncompromised Message.

Cast your mind back on how the Body of Christ's journey began. On the day the Church of Jesus Christ was birthed in the Holy Spirit in Acts 2, Peter spoke under the power of the Holy Spirit and on that day, three thousand believed in the Lord Jesus Christ, were baptised and were added to the one hundred and twenty who had received the promised Holy Spirit. It is what Peter said in conclusion of his preach, that I want to highlight, "The promise is for you and your children and for all who are far-off – for whom the Lord our God will call." [Acts 2: 39]. The Church was birthed with continuity at its very core. May Jesus Christ who lives in us, be seen, given to others, magnified and be at the very centre of each of our legacy.

May today mark a new season of your life. Go and become that which you were born to be. Fulfil your destiny. Do not waste another day and do not procrastinate. Give yourself wholly to God. Spend time in the Word; meditate on it, linger, regularly return to it, and memorise it. Put pressure on the Word and see what it will produce for you, in you and through you. Remember, you are a son or daughter of the kingdom of God. Earth must know you because you chose to be a building for God [John 14: 20]. Be filled with the Holy Spirit [Ephesians 5: 18]. Be a willing, yielded, and obedient vessel. Know Jesus intimately, walk with Him, talk to Him, and be led by His Holy Spirit daily. Be consumed by Him.

Align your vision, plans, and purpose to God's. Latch and be hooked onto God's purpose. For when you live in His purpose, you will permanently walk in the supernaturally ordinary realms of God [Acts 16: 17 – 18]. Be passionate, sharpen your spiritual perception, and be God's voice. Influence your sphere: friends, colleagues, neighbourhoods, nations, and generations. Learn from the past, live in the moment, and expect a better tomorrow. Finish your race strong and arrive in the presence of God having emptied your reserves.

Do not die young or prematurely. Instead, fulfil the number of days of your life. Live to a good old age only pointing to Jesus Christ. Leave a platform, a springboard, a permanent mark, and an enduring impression for others to emulate. Touch people for perpetuity. In turn, they too will walk with Jesus, make disciples, influence, inspire others, and change lives to the glory of God. Now, initiate, accelerate, transfer, and see God give the increase!

Leviticus 26: 9 - 10
I will look on you with favour and make you fruitful and multiply your numbers, and I will keep my covenant with you. You will still be eating last year's harvest when you will have to move it out to make room for the new.

Milton Keynes UK
Ingram Content Group UK Ltd.
UKHW020653191023
430917UK00014B/489